Every great oak was once a little nut that stood its ground.

Every great oak was
once a little nut that
stood its ground.

Trudi's Garden

The Story of Trudi Temple, Founder of Market Day

Phlox (*P. paniculata* seedling)
Day Lily (*Hemerocallis* 'Jungle Beauty')

Trudi with Tulips (*Tulipa* 'Spring Green')

Trudi's Garden

The Story of Trudi Temple, Founder of Market Day

Trudi R. Temple (signature)

LAURIE BOHLKE
& TRUDI TEMPLE

Photography by
Gail Perkins

Foreword by
Debra Landwehr Engle

Goblin Fern Press, Inc.
3809 Mineral Point Road
Madison, WI 53705

Publisher's Cataloging-In-Publication Data
(Prepared by The Donohue Group, Inc.)

Bohlke, Laurie.
    Trudi's garden : the story of Trudi Temple, founder of Market Day / Laurie Bohlke & Trudi Temple; photography by Gail Perkins ; foreword by Debra Landwehr Engle.—1st edition

        p. 192 : ill. ; 25.4 x 20.32 cm.
    Includes bibliographical references and index.
    ISBN-13: 978-1-59598-026-7
    ISBN-10: 1-595-98026-1

1. Temple, Trudi. 2. Market Day (Firm)--History. 3. Women gardeners--Illinois--Biography. 4. Women immigrants--Illinois--Biography. 5. Businesswomen--Illinois--Biography. 5. Cooperative marketing of farm produce--Illinois--History. I. Temple, Trudi. II. Perkins, Gail L., 1944- III. Engle, Debra Landwehr. IV. Title.

SB63 .T46 2006
635/.092 2005921388

The names of several people in Trudi's life have been changed.
The photographers of the uncredited black-and-white images are unknown.
Book design: Paetzold Associates, Saint Charles, Illinois
Indexing by Willard & Associates, Madison, WI

Published by Goblin Fern Press, Inc., 3809 Mineral Point Road, Madison, WI 53705
www.goblinfernpress.com Toll-free: 888-670-BOOK (2665)

Printed in the United States of America

The entrance to Trudi's home

Dedication

I dedicate this book to the most wonderful

country I know, where I have been privileged

to live for more than forty years—a land where

creativity is encouraged, dreams come true

and freedom is not harnessed—

The United States of America.

Trudi R. Temple

TABLE OF CONTENTS

Preface

The boulder garden

Isn't that Trudi Temple running toward me?

I was walking in a local forest preserve when Trudi approached, running at a healthy clip. How typical—the Trudi I had met on the tennis court years earlier attacked that game and everything else in her life full speed ahead. Since our tennis days, we each had taken our lives in new directions. She concentrated on her garden and the expansion of Market Day, and I became a nature photographer. Our chance meeting that morning in 1998 led to the book you now hold in your hands.

As we walked and chatted that day, Trudi generously offered her garden to me and my camera. Trudi's garden immediately became my studio. Trudi often worked in the garden while I photographed. She told me that Margo and Trudianne wanted her to write down her stories—the bedtime stories of their youth. Her daughters hoped to share them with their own children, to capture the same turn of a phrase and twinkle of mischief they had heard at bedtime over the years.

Initially, Trudi's busy schedule left no room for such an undertaking. However, dramatic changes in her life quickly made the writing of those stories a priority. I offered my images as meager thanks for her open invitation to photograph in her garden. The casual "stories just for the girls" became "Why don't we write a book?" Trudi doesn't do anything in a small way. If she could dream it, we could do it.

It was about that time Laurie Bohlke moved to Illinois and was introduced to me by my photography mentor, her brother, David Middleton. Laurie, with her organizational and literary skills, completed the team. She is the leader who has kept two dreamers on course.

Thank you, Trudi and Laurie, for enriching my life.

Gail Perkins

Gail and I arrive at Trudi's house for a meeting and ring the doorbell. There's no answer. We're not surprised and head to the garden.

There's Trudi, walking toward the house from her caged vegetable garden, carrying a basket overflowing with vegetables. She is dressed in faded jeans and a pink knit shirt, with her long hair swirled into a casual topknot. After completing a routine ten-hour day in her garden, she shows no sign of fatigue. She smiles and hugs us.

As we approach Trudi's back door, we walk past a large wooden bowl filled with orange rinds, carrot tops, apple cores and other unidentifiable kitchen remnants, destined for one of her celebrated "Trudi pits." Before she invites us inside, Trudi steps out of her garden clogs and places them neatly by the door.

We climb the short flight of stairs to her country kitchen. Light streams in from the large window over the sink, illuminating Trudi's collection of antique teapots perched on the window ledge. On this cool fall evening, something smells heavenly. I glance around the room and find a giant soup pot sitting on the stove. Next to the sink, a wooden chopping block stands ready. Trudi quickly chops vegetables and adds them to the simmering soup broth. Soon we'll be savoring her flavorful "Just Wing It" vegetable soup.

Ever hospitable, Trudi prepares three giant mugs of apricot tea and offers us bowls of freshly picked raspberries. We settle on wooden chairs at her long trestle table, and I start my tape recorder.

Years later, as I anticipate holding the completed book in my hands, I marvel at our journey together. What a blessing it's been to know and love Trudi and Gail.

Laurie Bohlke

The pond garden

Foreword

Trudi Temple knows how to make life work. Her guidelines for living include charity and forgiveness, service to others, and persistence, persistence, persistence. Those are my words, not hers. And believe me, her words are much more eloquent.

I first met Trudi when I was researching gardeners for my book, *Grace from the Garden: Changing the World One Garden at a Time*. I'd been referred to her by a fellow writer who had interviewed her for a magazine article. Knowing that I was looking for gardeners who had a sense of service and mission, he told me about Trudi. "She lives in Hinsdale, Illinois," he said. "She has the most beautiful gardens. But she also started a program called Market Day."

When I called Trudi, I was greeted by a German accent and a lilting voice. She sounded welcoming. Not exactly like an old friend, but like someone who has an abundant spirit with more than enough to share.

"Could I come interview you for the book?" I asked.

"Yes," she said. "Certainly. Come, and I'll show you my gardens."

And so I drove to Hinsdale, Illinois, pulled up in front of a half-timbered house and met Trudi in her backyard. This, I discovered, was no ordinary yard. And Trudi, I soon found out, was no ordinary gardener.

Wearing a sweatshirt, with her hair pulled up in a bun, Trudi took me on a tour of her own private park, where a path of grass wove between perfect beds of perennials and annuals. It was a morning in early May, and it seemed as though her entire yard was in bloom. She had pruned trees into interesting shapes, fertilized plants with her own blend of compost and started her own nursery at the back of the yard, where she stuck plants in pots in the ground and raised them until they could be transplanted.

This was story enough—a self-taught gardener who had developed countless techniques for making gardening easier and more fruitful. But that was only part of Trudi's story. Over lunch—a soup made from her homegrown vegetables—she recounted several life experiences and I started to understand the rest.

Bleeding Heart (*Dicentra spectabilis* 'Alba')

Trudi approaches life as a garden, an opportunity to nurture and tend people as well as plants. Her concern for the welfare of others began in her childhood, when she grew up in war-torn Germany. It continued to grow when she immigrated to the United States and married, traveling all over the world and seeing the dire need of people in other countries. Ultimately, it resulted in the development of Market Day, a one-of-a-kind school fundraising program that, over the past thirty years, has raised more than $330 million for schools across the country.

On that May day, I started to understand a few important things about Trudi Temple. For instance, many people have ideas; Trudi has a vision. She sees a problem as an opportunity for a solution, and the solution probably will exceed everyone's expectations. Many people have stories; Trudi has a legacy. Her gardens and mission work have dramatically altered the lives of more people than she will ever know. Many people have beliefs; Trudi has a philosophy. Her guidelines for living a successful life encompass service, work, self-esteem, beauty and respect. In short, Trudi is the go-to person, the one who will not only get things done, but will find a way to transcend the ordinary in the process.

Since the publication of *Grace from the Garden*, I've had the pleasure of visiting again with Trudi, and with Laurie Bohlke and Gail Perkins, who have worked for years on preparing this book. Every time I talk with Trudi, I learn something new, whether it's about gardening or about life.

She thinks big, has boundless energy and proves that one person can change the world. I am grateful to her, and to Laurie and Gail for bringing her entire story to you. Consider this book a tour through her gardens on a May morning, a conversation over lunch about what's important to her, a handbook for living a life that works. Trudi's story inspires and encourages, helping us all feel that anything is possible.

Debra Landwehr Engle

December 2004

Welcome

The lawn has been swallowed up, replaced by a garden paradise. In front of Trudi's house, a profusion of bright blossoms greets us as we walk up the Wisconsin limestone boulder path and pause near the friendship gate. Trudi smiles warmly as she opens the gate and invites us into her garden . . . and into her life.

Stone wall near Trudi's garage

PART ONE

CHILDHOOD OF LOVE AND WAR

Blue Holly (*Ilex x meserveae* 'Blue Prince')
Blue Spruce (*Picea pungens* 'Fat Albert')
Canna Lily (*C. edulis* 'Pretoria')
Hakone Grass (*Hakonechloa macra* 'Aureola')

Planting Seeds

Hakone Grass (*Hakonechloa macra* 'Aureola')

With her *Reichsmarks* tucked in her pocket, six-year-old Trudi walked three kilometers to the Sandhofen stationery store. The owner, an old lady wearing a black dress and faded apron, looked up from her figuring when the little girl pushed open the door. Trudi, just big enough to look over the counter, asked for colored pencils.

The woman peered over her glasses at Trudi. "Sorry, no colored pencils today."

"When will you have them? Maybe next week?" Trudi asked politely.

"Maybe," she answered, shifting her attention to an adult customer.

The next week Trudi again walked to the store. "Have you any colored pencils?"

"No, we still don't have any." The owner turned around and disappeared into the back room.

The third week Trudi asked, "Colored pencils?"

Glaring at her, the owner replied, "No."

Trudi had asked everyone in her small German village of Blumenau for colored pencils, but ended up drawing pictures with a few used stubs, not at all her fantasy. She coveted a set of perfect long pencils in varied colors.

Junghans, the grocery store across the street from Trudi's house, supplied the village's daily needs. For anything else, the villagers had to travel to Sandhofen, a town with paved sidewalks and numerous stores. Her country, however, was enmeshed in World War II and few frivolities were available; even necessities such as food and shoes were rationed.

After three weeks of trudging back and forth to Sandhofen, Trudi was willing to buy anything similar to a colored pencil set, but the store shelves were empty. Then she remembered how her mother had solved the problem of outgrown shoes. With most of the leather reserved for the war effort, each person was allotted only enough shoe stamps to buy one pair of shoes a

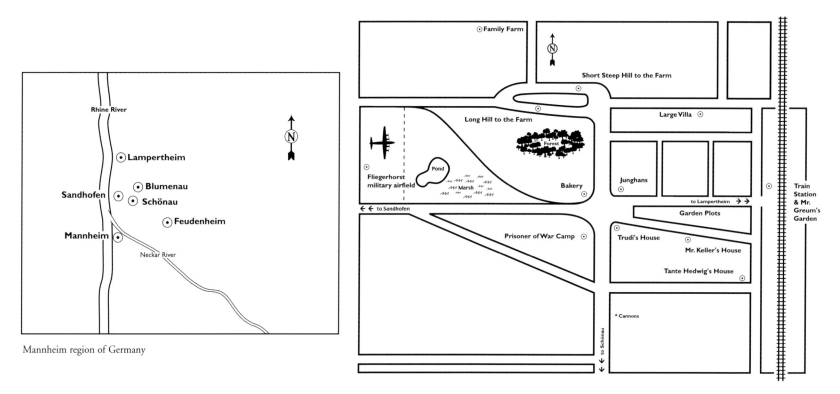

Mannheim region of Germany

Village of Blumenau

World War II 1938–1942

1938–1939

The hardships of war began with Hitler's aggressive expansion campaign to invade and conquer Austria, Czechoslovakia and Poland.

1940

Mussolini's Italy joined Hitler's war against Britain and France. The Axis forces conquered Denmark, Norway, Luxembourg, the Netherlands and Belgium. After France surrendered in June, Germany spent the next five months bombing Britain. The British resisted valiantly, and by October, it was clear that Hitler's plan to invade England had failed.

1941

After Greece and Yugoslavia were conquered, Russia was next. Hitler ignored their non-aggression pact and invaded in June. A secret alliance with Japan led Hitler to applaud the attack on Pearl Harbor in December. The United States entered the war.

1942

By the time Trudi harvested her beans, the world headlines had changed. Even though German U-boats still dominated the Atlantic and the African campaign was succeeding, grim news arrived from the eastern front in Russia; German forces were decimated at Stalingrad.

American and British pilots participated in their first joint bombing raids in Germany.

year. To make room for Trudi's growing toes, her mother cut holes in the tips of the shoes, exposing the open edges. She decorated these so artistically that Trudi received many compliments.

Trudi's mother, Anna, quickly came up with the answer to her pencil problem. "*Trudl*, your beans are ready in the garden. Pick them and take them to the store. Instead of giving the owner your worthless *Reichsmarks*, show her your beans and see what happens."

> Trudi's heart stood still.

For as long as she could remember, Trudi had watched and helped her mother in her garden. Her favorite part was picking the earliest vegetable, plump red radishes that puckered her mouth with sharp flavor. She even helped her mother plant flowers in the two new courtyard garden beds. In the spring of 1942, Anna gave Trudi a ten-foot-square garden plot, cleverly placed in the front corner of their yard. It would be hers alone. In addition to flowers, Trudi chose vegetables that were her favorites—radishes, peas, carrots and beans. Since most villagers had to walk by Trudi's garden to shop at *Junghans*, Trudi tried to keep her garden neat.

Leaning over the picket fence, the adults enjoyed watching her progress and admired her flowers and vegetables. Their sad, wartime expressions changed into smiles as they chatted with her. Already aware that a smile was much nicer to receive than a frown, Trudi delighted in cheering them up.

Clutching her paper sack full of green beans, Trudi's grey eyes twinkled and her blond braids bounced as she skipped down the country road. She entered the store for the fourth time and asked the shopkeeper, "Do you have colored pencils this week?"

"You were just in here last week," she frowned. "No colored pencils."

"Wait. Look at my beans. I just picked them today." The bag rustled invitingly as Trudi opened it.

The woman peered into the bag. The beans, bright green and crisp, were just as fresh as possible. Looking down at Trudi, she raised her index finger and said, "Just a moment." Then she disappeared through a curtain into the back room.

Trudi's heart stood still. She could hardly breathe as she heard boxes being thumped and shuffled. Had her mother's idea worked? When the owner reappeared, she was carrying a wonderful box of colored pencils. How thrilling! Trudi had made her first business deal and couldn't wait to tell her mother and her brother, Rudi.

The shopkeeper and the six-year-old developed a close relationship, with Trudi trading most of her vegetables, including some from her mother's garden, for toys and other back-room treats. After a while, the owner allowed Trudi into the back room to choose from her stock. Her favorite treasures were colorful, glass-beaded doilies shaped like flowers and stars.

Her mother's wisdom sparked Trudi's two lifelong passions, gardening and business. As a child, she liked business best and was always dreaming up ways to make money. When a long line of women shoppers waited outside *Junghans*, busy mothers who lived nearby paid her a few *Pfennige* to stand in line for them. As soon as Trudi stepped inside the store, they'd arrive to take her place.

She picked and sold whatever fruits or vegetables were in season, including strawberries from the fields and mushrooms from nearby woods. She gathered nettles for farmers' geese, dandelions for their rabbits and kindling for villagers' woodstoves. One of her favorite jobs was raking the mud sidewalks and making creative designs. Some villagers even detoured into the street to avoid destroying her artwork.

Anna

Emil

Tante Elise and
Onkel Schoh

Trudi smiles as she relates these stories about her early childhood, recalling happy times with her mother and older brother, Rudi. She has few memories of her father. He was drafted and began serving in the war in 1939, when Trudi was only three years old. He did come home on leave in 1942 for the holidays and a big New Year's Eve party. All the children were allowed to stay up late that night and celebrate with the houseful of family, neighbors and friends.

Trudi had no idea what was wrong…

Suddenly there was a weird sound—a loud, screaming noise overhead. Trudi's father reacted first and yelled, "Down! Cover your heads!" The adults shielded the children as everyone dove for the floor. They cringed as the horrible whistling sound passed overhead. Trudi had no idea what was wrong, but she knew the adults were panic-stricken.

Total silence. Nothing happened. Trudi's father ordered everyone to jump out of the window at the opposite end of the house and gather at the train station five blocks away. They waited there while he investigated.

Finally her father reappeared and explained the mystery. Her mother had saved their lives when she redesigned their tile courtyard and created two flower beds with fine, loose soil. A bomb had come in at an angle and buried its detonator in the soft soil—not yet frozen that winter. As the party-goers filed into the courtyard, the light of Trudi's father's flashlight illuminated the bomb.

The next day Trudi's father refused any help as he silently stuffed the bomb into a gunnysack, slung it over his shoulder and climbed onto his bicycle. He carefully rode out of town to their farm to detonate it. Back home, he proudly showed his family the spot behind his ear where a piece of shrapnel had hit him, even though he had hunkered down in a drainage ditch.

The bomb, huge to six-year-old Trudi, must have been one of the smallest used in World War II, since few bombs were light enough to be carried by one man. It was probably dropped from a British Royal Air Force plane, since the R.A.F. did most of its bombing runs over Germany at night. During their daytime attacks, the Americans had long-range fighter escorts to protect their bombers from the German *Messerschmidt* fighters.

Trudi loved to hear her parents tell stories about the years before the war—before she was born. In 1929, her father, Emil, a footloose twenty-two-year-old botanist, went to Munich to seek his fortune. An idealistic Marxist, his motto was "One for all and all for one." If necessary, he would give away his own clothing to help someone in need. Emil and his friends heard Adolph Hitler speak and quickly became disillusioned with the dictator's Nazi ideology. Plotting against him, Emil ended up in jail for several months after a friend's betrayal. In those early years, Hitler's critics still had a chance to walk away with their lives, but Nazi party agents watched Emil closely for years.

Soon after Emil was released from jail, he met Anna, a petite brunette. They often laughed over a story from their dating days. At a dance, Anna had felt the elastic waist of her half-slip give way and begin a slow slide down her legs. Showing amazing composure, she calmly stepped out of the slip and threw it out an open window. After a short courtship, Anna, who dreamed of being a ballerina, gave up that idea to marry Emil in 1930.

When a flower meadow outside of Mannheim became the new farming commune, Blumenau, Emil was offered a job. Since World War I, one method the German government had used to fight rampant inflation and the scarcity of jobs was to lease unused land to farmers and loan them money to build houses. Emil became general manager of the community of thirty-six families. Each family bought half of a duplex home in the town. The swamp outside Blumenau was drained and divided into farms for the villagers. After the produce was taken to the large collection hall across the street from Emil and Anna's house, it was sold in Mannheim and other nearby villages.

Community garden

Tante Elise's Apple Cake

1½ cups flour
2 t. baking powder
½ t. salt
½ cup sugar
1 stick butter or margarine
½ cup cold milk
1 egg
5 large cooking apples
¼ cup raisins (optional)

Topping
½ t. cinnamon
¼ cup sugar

1. Stir together flour, baking powder, salt and ½ cup sugar in a large bowl.

2. Melt butter or margarine in small pot over low heat. Remove pot from heat; add milk and egg. Beat with wire whisk.

3. Add butter mixture to dry ingredients. Mix well.

4. Spread dough evenly in a greased, 9-inch springform pan.

5. Peel and core apples; cut each into 8 sections. Arrange on top of dough. Sprinkle with ¼ cup raisins (optional).

6. Mix cinnamon with ¼ cup sugar in a small bowl. Sprinkle evenly over apples.

7. Bake at 350°F for at least one hour. Insert a toothpick into the center of cake to test for doneness. When the cake is done, the toothpick will come out clean.

8. Cool before removing from springform pan.

Serves 8—Delicious with whipped cream or ice cream.

Anna, Rudi, Trudi, *Onkel* Schoh, *Tante* Elise

Anna's oldest sister, Elise, and her husband, Johannes, moved into the other half of the duplex. After Trudi's brother, Rudi, was born in 1931, Johannes (*Onkel* Schoh) gave up orthopedic shoe-making for farming, bringing him closer to the family. Since Elise and Schoh couldn't have children, they doted on Rudi. Elise babysat for Rudi while Anna worked on the farm.

The initial success of the Marxist village didn't last long. By the time Trudi was born in 1936, the farmers had either become independent, as her family had, or had failed to make a living.

❧

One of Trudi's earliest memories is from the spring of 1941, when she was five. She loved the town's tradition on the day before Easter. The children went to the woods and gathered plant material—moss, flowers, soft little leaves—to make nests for the Easter Bunny. Trudi knew her mother's garden was the perfect place for him to visit; she tucked her nests under bushes, next to fence posts, in any cozy place.

Her mother, pleased with Trudi's industry, smiled and asked, "Where did you put them, *Trudl*? Show me your little hiding places."

The next morning Trudi ran to the garden. Sure enough, the Easter Bunny had found every nest and filled them with colored eggs. Then her mother made a special treat, delicious deviled eggs.

Trudi and Rudi agreed that their mother and *Tante* Elise were the best cooks in the world. As soon as Trudi came home from school, her first order of business was to find out what *Tante* Elise was having for dinner. Although neither family had a telephone, they had a common broom closet wall that separated the two houses. Trudi would go into the closet and bang on the wooden frame with a broomstick. Whap, whap, whap—three bangs were her call sign. Sometimes she missed the wood and left big gouges in the plaster. When her annoyed mother pointed out the damage, Trudi assured her that Rudi had put them there. He never complained and quietly patched them up.

After the three bangs, Trudi put her ear to the wall and waited. The broom closet on the other side of the wall opened with a delightful squeak. *Tante* Elise's voice called out, "*Ja, Trudl?*" and Trudi asked what she was cooking for supper. Her mother often made *Eintopf*, a stovetop meal all in one pot, or boiled potatoes served with pickled herring, cheese or molasses. As the war deteriorated, they had meat and dessert only on Sundays, but *Tante* Elise made gravy that tasted just like meat. *Tante* Elise was a more sophisticated cook. Trudi particularly loved her *Schupfnudel*, a tasty potato dumpling rolled out like a sausage, boiled in salty water and served with sauerkraut or a little gravy. Her favorite dessert was *Tante* Elise's apple cake.

Tante Elise's dinner was usually the better choice because, when Trudi asked her mother about dinner plans, many times Anna was deeply involved in a book and replied, "Don't know yet." She was easygoing, creative, adventurous and disorganized; her love of reading often caused chaos. Losing track of time, she often threw dinner together at the last minute and left the kitchen in a mess.

> ...the dead bugs would come to life...

Even beyond cooking styles, Anna and Elise were total opposites. Strict and formal, Elise wore one apron for working around the house and another for cooking. She changed her clothes into a high-necked, long-sleeved, black dress for supper. To serve the meal, she protected her dress with a third white apron, then removed it when she sat down. Trudi liked her neat, organized style.

Tante Elise didn't always like Trudi's style, though. Her dining room table was covered with a tempting tablecloth edged with long gold fringes reaching almost to the floor. Fascinated by those silky threads, Trudi couldn't resist hiding under the table and braiding them over and over. The next thing *Tante* Elise knew, her tablecloth had braids as high as Trudi's fingers could reach. After she undid all of Trudi's hard work, the kinky fringes didn't hang straight. *Tante* Elise scolded her, finally threatening that if the fringes were braided one more time, Trudi would have to eat in the kitchen by herself.

Trudi ate many solitary meals.

Onkel Willi

Trudi didn't see her other aunts and uncles as often, although her father's sister, Hedwig, and her husband, Adolf, lived just a block away. Her mother's youngest brother, Willi, and his wife, Liesel, lived in nearby Feudenheim, another village outside Mannheim. Willi was the naturalist in the family, as well as a talented musician, first-rate athlete and great joker. Shadow boxes full of his insect collection lined the walls of the dark, nightmarish bathroom at Trudi's *Oma's* (Grandma's) house. Trudi was petrified the dead bugs would come to life, leap out of the boxes and attack before she ran the gauntlet back and forth to the toilet. And she never returned to *Onkel* Willi's bedroom after she saw his lamp made from a human skull.

In 1943, at the age of seven, Trudi walked to the farm to help with chores—after her homework was done. During the wheat harvest, she was proud of her important job. When the inefficient threshing machines littered the ground with spilled wheat, Trudi and her friends salvaged baskets of wheat from the nearby farms.

Struby, her little schnauzer, and her green baby carriage always accompanied Trudi to the farm. She'd pile her books, toys and Struby into the carriage for the two-kilometer walk down the steep hill out of the village. On the way to the farm, she passed the woods next to Fliegerhorst, the military airfield. Opposite the woods, the wealthiest family in town lived on a twenty-acre estate with a large house, beautiful gardens and popular restaurant. Before the war, people drove out from Mannheim for fine dining in the country. During the war, with money scarce, the restaurant was boarded up.

One day at school, while thinking of the long walk to the farm, Trudi came up with a novel idea and decided to try it that afternoon. Leaving Struby and all her belongings at home, she walked to the top of the hill and climbed into the baby carriage. With a push, it started going faster and faster—a thrilling ride until it hit a rock. Trudi flew out onto the deserted road, sat up and started crying. Her knees, embedded with gray specs of gravel, were covered with blood. With everyone at the farm, no one could help her. She limped all the way to her mother's arms.

Seeing Trudi's bloody legs, Anna simply asked, "How did you manage this one?"

❧

Trudi remembers that her mother loved to laugh—despite the hardships and sorrows of the war. They rarely heard from Emil, an Army truck driver who ferried supplies to the front near Stalingrad. Schoh had served in the German Army cavalry before he developed a severe case of bleeding ulcers and was sent home. Their family was heartbroken to learn that Willi and his entire Army unit had been killed in the Russian campaign.

Mourning for Willi and worrying about her absent husband weren't the only burdens Anna had to bear. She was responsible for raising her two children and running the farm. Somehow she managed to get things done with creativity and flair, even making stylish new clothes out of their old ones. Trudi had an entire outfit made from old curtains, the blouse from the sheers and the skirt from the drapes. Anna even unraveled old sweaters and added new yarn to knit new striped ones.

Anna constantly struggled to grow enough food—not only to feed her family, but also to barter on the black market, where she obtained luxuries such as herring, extra sugar and chocolate.

She raised chickens, ducks and rabbits for meat and even kept a secret pig hidden in the back corner of her greenhouse under a workbench. By law, all farm animals had to be registered and a portion given to the government inspector on his surprise visits. With enough food and space for only one pig, Anna was determined not to give up any meat. It was for her family, period.

When the pig was ready to be butchered, Schoh volunteered to shoot it. Anna's job was to hold the pig's snout with a rope. To camouflage the noise, they waited for the sirens announcing an air raid, certain everyone would be in shelters. The siren sounded along with the bang of Shoh's homemade execution device. To their horror, it misfired, only wounding the pig, which immediately started squealing loudly. Panicked, Anna grabbed the pig's snout tighter, holding on until it suffocated.

> Anna's job was to hold the pig's snout with a rope.

After the pork loins were carved out, every other usable part of the pig was processed into headcheese, a loaf of seasoned, jellied meat. Trudi and the rest of the family thought that it was the best headcheese they had ever eaten. Anna wouldn't eat any and never raised another pig.

While Trudi's mother focused on providing food for her family, seven-year-old Trudi was more interested in having fun. To her, going fast was exhilarating, but her scooter was too slow and her roller skates didn't work on the gravel roads to the farm. One day, she remembered the bicycle *Tante* Elise had tucked away in her shed. Waiting until her aunt wasn't home, Trudi dug out that old bicycle and dragged it to the nearby woods. Too small to reach the seat, she wedged herself under the bicycle's bar, reached up to the handlebars and leaned to one side. By angling the bicycle away for balance, Trudi taught herself to ride.

Trudi's fun ended the day a neighbor saw her and told Anna, "Your daughter has a huge bicycle over in the woods and is trying to ride it." Anna firmly told Trudi there would be no more riding until she could sit on the seat. Determined to resume her bike-riding adventures, Trudi dutifully followed her mother's orders. But when she climbed onto the seat, her feet couldn't reach the foot pedals, where the brakes were located.

Undaunted, Trudi found a perfect place to ride—on a different road out to the farm. Instead of the short, steep hill where she had fallen out of the baby carriage, she walked the bike to the top of a longer, gentler hill. After pushing off and leaping onto the seat, Trudi had a lovely, long ride down the hill. She knew that the bicycle would finally slow down by itself as the road flattened.

One day Farmer Gifhorn pushed his bike and a cart full of vegetables around the bend and up the same hill—just as Trudi flew down the hill. No time for Trudi to stop or steer around him. He looked up the hill in horror, dropped everything and ran up the embankment.

She missed him, but smashed into the cart. Vegetables went one way and Trudi the other, as red and white cabbages, celery root and carrots rolled down the hill behind her. Farmer Gifhorn came running over to the spot where she lay on the gravel road. He wasn't mad, just concerned about Trudi. Although she had scrapes all over, she quickly jumped up and said, "I'm all right; I'm all right." He looked her over and sent her home.

The next day he carted the twisted, wrecked bicycle to her house. Both Trudi's mother and *Tante* Elise were exasperated with her and her never-ending exploits. Frowning, her mother said, "Well, now you've done it, *Trudl*! You've made a royal mess of this bike."

Trudi was quite a trial to her mother. Yet, in an era of frequent corporal punishment, Anna only struck her once. Trudi's most dreaded household chore was washing Rudi's socks. Even though she knew laundry was a woman's job in her family, Trudi didn't understand why he couldn't wash his own things. Home from school one day, she was greeted by a disgusting, dirty heap of socks soaking in the washtub. Instead of sitting down to do her homework and washing the repulsive socks, she escaped to the train station. Without telephones to call each other, she and her buddies knew they would meet at the station when their chores and homework were completed.

Trudi had been there only a few minutes when she felt a hard tug on her braids. Rudi stood behind her, frowning. "Mama sent me. You've got to come home right away."

Trudi knew she was in trouble and, as soon as she walked in, her mother grabbed her, swinging a wet wool sock at her head. While her head was buffeted by a sock beating, Trudi endured a lecture about responsibility.

Trudi remembers her response, "Pouting, I washed all the darn things."

Despite her mischief, Trudi passionately wanted to help her family survive the war. One brainstorm involved old Mr. Greum, who lived across the tracks from the train station. When a train was due, his job was to turn the wheel that brought down the barrier across the road. In the fall, the large hazelnut bush in his yard, heavy with nuts, drooped over the fence. In the morning before school, Trudi would run over to see if any hazelnuts had fallen. Her mother told her she could take only the ones on the sidewalk, outside his garden fence. Although powerfully tempted to reach past the picket fence to collect forbidden hazelnuts, Trudi usually restrained herself.

Year after year Trudi picked sidewalk hazelnuts until one day she was startled when the entire bush shook vigorously. Hazelnuts rained down by the hundreds. Mr. Greum had been watching her and decided to reward her industriousness. He even brought out a little basket and helped Trudi pick up her windfall.

❧

Until the bombing became a daily danger, the entire village was a playground for Trudi and her friends. They roamed freely, making up games, including a special game during the fall harvest. An old bearded farmer on his way to the sugar mill drove a big wagon loaded with

You are a thief.

sugar beets through the village. Swaying his body in step with the oxen, he sat slumped over the reins with a cap pulled low over his wrinkled face. Scruffy and sleepy, the farmer never paid attention, never even looked up when one of Trudi's friends figured out that he could jump onto the cart and steal sugar beets. Soon it became a game for all the children to steal beets and take them home to their mothers.

Trudi loved bringing those beets home because she was helping. Her mother would say, "Oh no, you should not do this. You are a thief." Then she'd take the first beet and scrub it. "You must never do this again." Anna eagerly chopped more beets and dropped them into the pot. Rules were different during the war years, and Trudi knew her mother was delighted to make molasses, one of the staples of their wartime meals.

On molasses days, the house was warm and fragrant as the beets boiled for hours in pots of water. Then the syrupy water was strained, boiled down to become molasses, poured into every available jar and stored in the basement. As food supplies dwindled, Trudi's family ate molasses, the only available source of unrationed sugar, with bread and potatoes.

Those precious molasses containers faced a tragic fate as the war intensified.

GARDEN TIP

Digging and filling a "Trudi Pit"

"Trudi Pits"

As an adult carrying on the love of gardening that sustained her as a child, Trudi has developed her own techniques to nurture her exquisite gardens. In early summer, when the Astilbes are in full bloom, visitors to Trudi's garden are often amazed to see these shade-loving plants flourishing in full sun. When they ask how it's possible, Trudi gives them a simple answer: "It's the ground they grow in." The Astilbes, along with the other plants in her garden, benefit from her unique composting system that a visiting garden group from St. Louis named "Trudi Pits."

Here's how you can make your own pits:

Dig a deep hole—big or small, it doesn't matter. Three feet by three feet is ideal, but you may have room for only a one-foot by one-foot hole.

Throw in decomposable things: garden debris including weeds and twigs, junk mail, cardboard and kitchen scraps. Avoid meat products that will attract carnivores. Fill the hole to ground level.

Top the hole with six to eight inches of soil from the next hole you dig; then set a stepping stone, wood round, or garden planter on it to mark the spot.

The following spring, or at least six months later, remove the marker and add more soil to fill the indentation. This rich soil is ready for planting.

The many benefits include no unsightly area in the garden and no laborious distribution from aboveground compost piles. Best of all, plants will thrive in several feet of great soil, not just a few inches of top dressing. Trudi concludes, "Plants become more disease-resistant, healthier looking and a pleasure for any gardener."

Peony (*Paeonia* 'Friendship')
Snowdrop Anemone *(Anemone sylvestris)*

Prisoners of War

Bleeding heart (*Dicentra spectabilis*)

It is one thing to be a soldier, drafted or enlisted in the military to serve your country, and quite another to be a child caught in war, with bombs falling all around you and the safety of your home and family threatened in sunlight and in darkness.

For Trudi, war was the backdrop of childhood, the setting for grief and anguish, but also for strength of character and acts of heroism. In 1942, six-year-old Trudi was too young to understand about Hitler's war. She did understand perfectly that the beans she harvested and traded were a sweet and constant counterpoint to the changes she saw all around her.

In 1943, her worldview changed right outside her bedroom window when the village's produce collection hall became a prisoner-of-war (POW) camp. From her bedroom, she could peer into the scuffed-dirt courtyard of the camp. The first occupants were young Russian women with cropped hair, wearing long dark skirts, blouses and kerchiefs. As Trudi lay in bed, she heard their soft, mournful singing. When she walked to school, she looked through the tall barbed-wire fence, often giving them a shy smile. One Russian woman kept escaping, but she was always found near the village pond—on her knees, praying. Brought back to camp, she was locked up again behind the barbed wire. Without identification papers or money, the prisoners couldn't actually escape because there was nowhere to go.

One day, as suddenly as they had come, the Russian women vanished. Fierce-looking men from Mongolia wearing long black braids down their backs took the women's place. After a while, the Mongolians disappeared, and French and Polish men filled the camp, standing in the courtyard under the watchful eyes of the guards.

These prisoners interacted with Trudi, smiling and motioning to her as she walked by. Not understanding what they wanted, Trudi asked her mother, "Why do they point at our house?" Her mother walked outside, looked at the house and smiled. She had hung ears of corn under the eaves to dry until ready to be used as chicken feed. The men, desperately hungry, hoped Anna might share some.

She and Trudi obliged, devising a scheme to help the prisoners. Trudi hid a few ears under her coat, walked past the prisoners and then paused by the fence to pass the corn through the barbed wire. Although the guards must have caught on, they looked the other way, unwilling to arrest a child. Trudi knew this was her job; if Anna had tried it, she could have been imprisoned.

Surprisingly, that summer each family was allowed to choose a prisoner to work for them—as long as they fed him and brought him back to the camp at night. Trudi chose Friedrich, a handsome, blue-eyed, blond Frenchman. He stepped into the family and helped her mother with the household and garden chores. But one day in early fall, when Trudi and her mother crossed the street to pick him up, he wasn't there. He had vanished, just like the Russian women and the Mongolian men.

Trudi hid a few ears under her coat…

Despite these tribulations, Trudi's loving family gave her stability and the ability to see the best in everyone. She remembers most of the Nazis in Blumenau as decent people who simply belonged to the National Socialist Party. Mr. Klein, the one exception, lived on Trudi's street. He ordered the villagers to follow his commands, raising their right arm and yelling out, "*Heil* Hitler," instead of exchanging a gentle "*Guten Tag*." Elise was on his watch list because she was childless, making her a failure in the eyes of the Nazis, who demanded that German women have many children to carry on the Aryan race.

One day, an eighteen-year-old girl from the neighboring town rode her bicycle through Blumenau. Mourning the recent death of her father, she was dressed all in black. As she rode by the prisoner-of-war camp, one of the male prisoners said, "Hello."

"Hello," she replied.

That was all she said, but Mr. Klein witnessed the greeting. He pulled her off her bike, dragged her to his house and violently hacked off her hair, cutting her scalp repeatedly. Then he marched her through the streets. The villagers stared in horror at the blood running down her face as Mr. Klein forced her to ring her bicycle bell and call out, "I am a prisoner-of-war camp whore."

The outraged townspeople, too intimidated to protest, returned to their houses and silently closed their doors. The consequences of any complaint could have been deadly.

Trudi observed the impact of fear on human behavior, but she also knew the impact of love. Her mother's best friend was the only Jewish woman in town. Anna kept her friend's secret, protecting

World War II 1943

The Americans began bombing Germany in earnest.

The last German units surrendered to the Russians at Stalingrad. In July, the German forces began their final Russian initiative in a massive battle at Kursk. Although the Russians lost more men and military equipment, the German Army had no way to replenish its forces or supplies. After 330,000 Germans had been killed or captured in the Russian campaign, the German Army's long retreat from the disastrous Eastern front began.

Trudi's family and the three-wheeled truck

her from wearing a yellow star, from suffering escalating indignities and from being sent to a concentration camp.

Auschwitz and Birkenau concentration camps were about three hundred miles away, a distant threat. Industrial Mannheim, a bombing target, was much closer to home, but Fliegerhorst, the military airfield, was just four blocks away. During his trips to the Russian front, Emil worried about the constant danger his family faced. He had to find a way to keep his wife and children safe. When he met a family who lived near Gumbinnen, on the border of Prussia and Lithuania, he devised a plan. Emil frequently stayed overnight with the family, bringing gifts of elk he hunted and killed, honey he collected, and other delicacies he bartered for. In exchange, he asked them to offer sanctuary to his family if the war ever threatened the Rhine Valley.

In the fall of 1943, bombing increased on Fliegerhorst. The wailing sirens signaled incoming fear and destruction. These ominous sounds became imprinted on Trudi's mind. The first siren, a shrill whoop, traveled up and down the scale and warned of bombing. The second siren, a slower and deeper sound, signaled imminent bombing. Both brought the same message: drop everything and seek shelter.

In the basement with her relatives, Trudi knew enemy planes were launching flares to illuminate the ground, then swooping down to drop their bombs. As the house swayed from shock waves, Trudi was terrified and often wet her pants, fearing her family would be killed.

Eventually, a steady siren alerted them the bombing was over—at least for the time being.

For weeks the bombing raids intensified. Finally, Anna had had enough and decided it was time to seek refuge with the family in Prussia. Before leaving home, she wrapped most of the family's valuables in oiled paper and buried them in the ground. At that point in the war, the German Army confiscated any cars they could find, but Anna outwitted them. She unscrewed or removed everything she could from the family's three-wheeled truck, including the wheels and engine, burying these critical pieces. Only the truck's carcass remained in the yard.

> These ominous sounds became imprinted on Trudi's mind.

Anna packed small bags for herself, Rudi and Trudi. She comforted her children during the arduous three-day train ride to the remote rural town of Gumbinnen. In truth, she needed comforting herself; just before they fled, she learned that Emil was missing in Russia.

Germany 1943

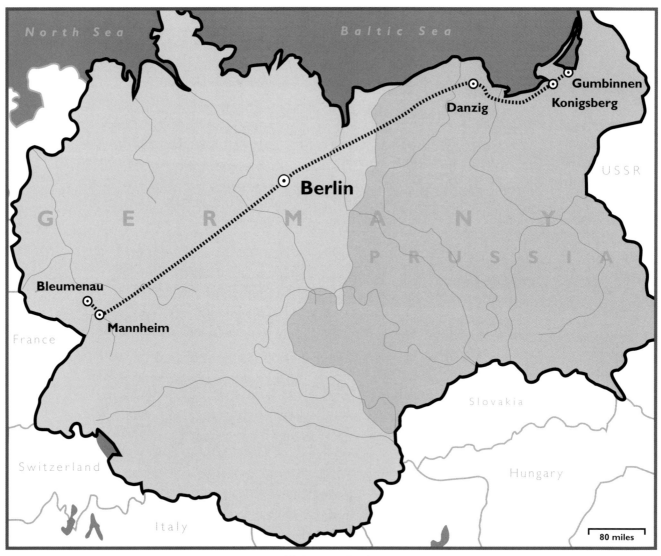

The journey to Prussia

The scarcity and fear of war brought out the worst in the Prussian family, particularly since they no longer received gifts from Emil. Furious about feeding three extra people, they rarely gave Trudi and her family anything but leftovers or mashed potatoes with mixed-in fried pork fat. Trudi and Rudi daydreamed about food; even molasses with potatoes began to sound delectable to them.

Winter set in with a frigid fury. Trudi, Anna and Rudi shared one bed—with the Prussian family's grumpy grandfather sleeping across the chilly room. All the bedding was infested with fleas. At night, Anna made a game out of finding fleas and throwing them at the snoring man's bed, as the children roared with laughter under the feather bed.

Trudi and Rudi were miserable in Prussia. With little to do, they played cards and wandered outside, where neighbor kids teased them about their unfamiliar dialect. Trudi had only one toy to play with, a celluloid doll with movable arms and legs.

On Christmas Eve, Trudi's family felt homesick and forlorn until a local woman who had befriended Anna invited them to her home. They walked down the snow-packed dirt road to the woman's cozy house. For Trudi, the highlight of the visit was the kind woman's parting gift; she sent them home with a bag of Christmas cookies.

Right after they stepped outside into the icy chill, Anna smiled and opened the bag. "We'll have to eat all these cookies before we get back, or that monstrous family will take them away from us." As the snow fell, the three walked along a silent farm road past a pine forest, stuffing themselves full of Christmas treats and enjoying a rare moment of contentment.

After the holidays, nothing could alleviate the misery of winter. Trudi begged her mother to go back home. "I'll never, ever wet my pants or be scared of the bombs or war again if you'll just take us home," she promised. Anna tried to buy tickets, but the trains were filled with terrified people escaping west, away from the bombarded eastern German cities and the advancing Russians. Trudi and her family were forced to endure the rest of the winter in Prussia.

> Trudi begged her mother to go back home.

In early spring, Anna finally secured tickets. They rode on an oxen cart to the train station. Soldiers and refugees lugging their sacks and packs jammed the train beyond capacity. Trudi, her mother and brother stood in the aisle for the first day's interminable journey, from Gumbinnen to Danzig. The second day, they boarded the train from Danzig to Berlin and found the crowding even worse. Thoroughly miserable, they stood again.

Sweet Autumn Clematis *(C. paniculata* 'Sweet Autumn'*)*

Chocolate *Busserl*, a chocolate cookie

¾ cup (1½ sticks) butter

1 cup sugar

5 cups hazelnuts, ground in a food processor into bread crumb consistency not as fine as powder

1¼ cups semisweet chocolate chips, ground into small slivers, not powdered

1. Cream butter and sugar together in large bowl. Add ground hazelnuts and chocolate. Mix well.

2. Cover dough and chill in refrigerator for 2 hours.

3. Form dough into small balls. Place on greased baking sheet.

4. Bake in 350°F. oven for 15 minutes. Bake on top rack to avoid burning the bottoms of the cookies.

5. Cool for 20 minutes on baking sheet before removing to wire rack.

Makes 4–5 dozen. These cookies freeze well and last a long time in a tin.
They are great for people with gluten intolerance, since the recipe contains no flour.

Anna had carefully packed provisions, but they ran out long before the trip ended on the third day. Nothing was left for them to eat or drink. A friendly soldier gave Trudi a red apple from his backpack. Hours later, a woman in a flowered dress placed Trudi on her lap next to the window. Drooping with pain and exhaustion, Trudi didn't speak—all she could think of was her thirst. When she saw drops of condensation rolling down the warm window, she leaned over and licked them, stealing moisture as the train rolled down the tracks toward home.

Trudi had turned into a different child by the time they returned home. Her innocence was replaced by determination. True to her word, she never feared bombs again, instead inventing a game to spot the lead airplane's flares. "Christmas trees," she and Rudi called them, as the light spread wider and wider until suddenly everything was illuminated.

The ground shook as the nearby airfield took hit after hit. The family farm, even closer to the airfield, was pockmarked with bomb craters. As they filled with groundwater, Trudi and Rudi turned them into swimming holes, jumping in and splashing around—defying danger.

The Nazi government asked teachers for help recovering bomb shrapnel. The students were instructed to hunt for the shards and made a game out of it. Who could collect the most? The teachers took the shrapnel to a collecting station to be melted into metal for the war effort.

> Her innocence was replaced by determination.

The war years demanded cleverness, resourcefulness and strength. They also required people to keep things to themselves. Adults drilled the importance of secrecy into Trudi and Rudi, telling them not to talk to anyone outside the family about private matters. The government reinforced that secrecy. All over town, posters of shadows with eyes warned the townspeople, "*Der Feind hört mit*." (The enemy listens.) For Trudi, this veil of silence became a habit.

Secrets can burden children, especially when faced with war's brutality. As eight-year-old Trudi wandered in the forest one day, she found a booklet. Propaganda leaflets often floated down from the sky and were collected to use as notepaper, toilet paper or kindling. But this time, the booklet was filled with color photos of concentration camp atrocities.

Trudi looked at each page and was sickened. Not wanting to upset her mother or Rudi, she hid the repulsive booklet under her mattress. Yet, she couldn't stop looking at it and thinking about the skeletal people with suffering eyes. Every time she sat down to a meal, she remembered the images and couldn't eat.

First her mother was puzzled, then frightened, by Trudi's personality change. Where had her sunny, gregarious little girl gone? Instead, this morose child spent hours in her room—without confiding in her mother. Anna tempted Trudi with her favorite meals, but Trudi wouldn't even eat chocolate.

As Trudi lost weight, her depression grew. The booklet's images kept her prisoner in her own mind. That evil booklet consumed her for months, until she made a decision far beyond her years. Realizing the booklet was tearing her apart, she ripped it into tiny pieces and stuffed them down the toilet.

Over time she recovered, but she never forgot.

GARDEN TIP

The Boulder Garden

Trudi decided to use large boulders as a foundation for an ambitious rock garden behind the house. Since the garden's narrow curves and stone paths prevented machinery from entering the backyard, four hard-working men used logs and muscle to roll the boulders into place. Trudi packed soil into the crevices of this boulder garden and planted conifers, shrubs and perennials to soften the stone. When completing the project, she said, "I now know how the pyramids were built."

The stunning large white flowers of *Clematis* 'Henryi,' framed by blue spruce, drape over the boulders in midsummer, creating the effect of a waterfall. Between the boulders, the spaces are decorated with the tiny yellow flowers of *Aurina saxatilis* 'Citrina,' reminding Trudi of the castle walls in Germany.

(See image of *Aurina saxatilis* 'Citrina' on next page.)

The boulder garden

Clematis *(C.* 'Henryi'*)*
Hakone Grass (*Hakonechloa macra* 'Aureola')

Basket of Gold (*Aurina saxatilis* 'Citrina')
Hosta (*H.* 'Fried Bananas')

Hiding Places

Intersectional Peony (*Paeonia* 'Bartzella')

After returning from Prussia, Anna sent Rudi to a rural boarding school near the Swiss border. But was that enough to keep him safe? She worried even more as he approached his thirteenth birthday that summer. German boys of thirteen were being conscripted into school military units and even sent to war. Anna knew the Nazis were searching for German youths everywhere. Determined not to let Rudi go to war at such a young age, she quietly brought him home again. Then she struggled with the dilemma of how to keep Rudi's presence a secret from their friends, as well as their enemies.

With the escalation of nighttime bombing in 1944, Anna faced an even more desperate decision. Hard of hearing, she didn't always wake up when the sirens started. She moved Trudi and Rudi to her room so Rudi could wake her when the cacophony began. Anna had to carry Trudi, a sound sleeper, to the basement during the bombing raids. By late spring, even Rudi started sleeping through the unending sirens. The constant bombardment and fear became too stressful for Anna and she decided it would be safer to move to the basement permanently.

The move seemed like great fun to Trudi. She thought of their three basement rooms as quite a palatial layout. The first room was used to store canned food, winter vegetables and fruit; the far side of the room was filled with the water pump and large piles of wood and coal. All the precious furniture and treasures they could not keep safe upstairs were in the second room, including the prized molasses jars. Trudi, Rudi and their mother lived in the third room.

After *Tante* Elise and *Onkel* Schoh also moved to their basement, they all chiseled a big hole in the brick wall between the living quarters. Trudi's favorite part of basement living was climbing right through the hole to visit. With culinary aromas wafting through the air, she no longer had to call over to *Tante* Elise to find out what was cooking.

Anna decided to enlist Elise and Schoh to help her build a secret room for Rudi by digging under the basement coal storage area. They constructed a six-foot by ten-foot space, reinforcing it with bricks—just enough room for a bed, bedside table and lamp. To camouflage the small opening, they rolled a heavy oak armoire in front of the hole, but left it at an angle to the wall. When visitors arrived, Rudi jumped into the hole, and the armoire was quickly rolled flat against the wall.

Rudi

World War II 1944

During the winter of 1944, the massive Allied bombing of Germany heavily damaged the German airfields and planes, severely depleting their air capability. In March, 660 American planes began their first bombing raid on Berlin. The assault on German cities continued almost every day, gradually weakening the German will to resist.

The Allies landed in Italy and captured Rome in June. D-day, launching the invasion of France, occurred on June 6. More than 175,000 Allied troops landed in Normandy, France, and began their march toward Germany two days later.

The Allies marched through France, liberating Paris in August. In December, German forces fought back in Belgium in the Battle of the Bulge. The Allies refused to surrender and launched a counterattack later that month.

Rudi, exceptionally patient, hid in that hole for nearly the entire last year of the war. Even though no German civilian was allowed to keep a radio, Rudi had one stashed in his hiding place. While learning English listening to the BBC, Rudi taught Trudi. Because it was too dangerous to walk to the schools, she missed third grade; the cellar became her schoolroom and the occupants her teachers.

"That year taught us to be comfortable outside our comfort zones," Trudi explains. "We just accepted what was happening; there was no other way. We were survivors. The war built our character and brought us even closer together as a family. Despite the war, there was still much love, laughter and excitement."

There was a strict rule not to disturb the blackout paper affixed to their shutters; no light was allowed to escape. Filled with curiosity, Trudi often peeked out the door at night to hear the faraway noises and see the bright, glowing lights of bombs exploding in Mannheim. Each morning the villagers emerged from their houses and gathered to take stock of any damage. The Allies tried to avoid the village and aimed quite accurately; few homes were hit.

The winter of 1945 brought new danger from phosphorus bombs raining down. They were designed to plunge into a building and set it on fire. From the basement, Trudi heard them popping on the deserted streets.

In early March, a phosphorus bomb hit the Lehnhard family's house, five blocks away. When it began to burn, the whole village grabbed their buckets and ran to help. Even the prisoners, unguarded during the day, went to the rescue. Rudi couldn't be held back, climbed out of his hole and raced off. Trudi wanted to go also, but her mother told her she was too little.

After a while, one of their favorite prisoners came running past their house yelling, "Rudi, Rudi hurt; Rudi hospital!"

Panicked, Trudi took off without telling her mother. Panting from fear and repeatedly slipping in the mushy snow, she ran five long blocks to the Lehnhards' burning house and gasped, "Where is my brother?"

Someone yelled to her, "He's in the hospital." Trudi had to reach him. She started running to the hospital in Schönau, two kilometers away. She ran about halfway before the cannons next to the road began a barrage of anti-aircraft fire. Shock waves picked her up and flung her hard across the street against a wall. Stunned, Trudi lay still on the ground.

Two Polish prisoners found her and dragged her back into town, with her feet barely touching the ground. When the bombing became too intense to proceed, they left Trudi in a villager's dark,

World War II 1945

By the end of January, the last German offensive was crushed. In early March, the American Army crossed the Rhine River at Remagen, three hundred kilometers from Blumenau. By March 25, all of the German forces had been driven east of the Rhine.

crowded basement and ran back to their camp. Finally, quiet returned and Trudi walked home to her desperate mother, who wept and hugged her all at the same time. "Don't you ever do that again!" she admonished Trudi.

Several hours later Rudi came home with a gauze bandage wrapped around his head. A bucket thrown down from the roof had struck him in the eye.

On the morning of March 26, 1945, two days after her ninth birthday, Trudi was lying in bed reading when a stray shell landed short of its target and hit their house. The huge explosion violently tore open the walls. Instantly dust and debris filled the air. The shell damaged the entire street side of the house, ripping a giant hole in the parlor wall and destroying many possessions. In the basement storage room, jars of home-canned food broke, spewing molasses, tomato shreds, pickle pulp and glass shards everywhere.

Slowly, the massive iron door that separated the basement storage room from the living area caved in over Trudi. As the bedstead twisted and bent under the weight of the door, she shot out of bed.

A German soldier who was standing guard at the prison camp across the street ran over and climbed into the wreckage to see if the family was all right. They were unhurt, but badly shaken. Ironically, one of Hitler's many laws had saved them. All basement windows were required to have a thick concrete block placed in front of them. Their block, standing as tall and wide as their cookstove, three feet by four feet by five feet, had absorbed the shell's explosion and saved their lives.

That was the last day of the war for Blumenau.

In the afternoon, knowing the Americans were approaching the village and believing all the German soldiers had fled, Anna gathered her courage and hung out her homemade white flag of surrender. Timing was critical; if a German soldier had seen the flag, she would have been shot to death. However, if she did not fly the flag, the liberating forces wouldn't know the family was peaceful.

Hearing sadistic Mr. Klein had disappeared, Rudi went outside to help *Onkel* Schoh stabilize the roof. Trudi, her mother and *Tante* Elise still hid in the basement, grit and dust from the blast clinging to their clothes. To begin the cleanup, they stepped cautiously over loose bricks, mortar and glass. In the storage room, Trudi's precious leftover birthday cake, a rich three-layer vanilla torte, was now decorated with jagged needles of glass.

An odd sound in the distance grabbed their attention. The squeaking, screeching and grinding grew louder. Trudi's family, accustomed to many sounds of war, wasn't bothered by most unusual mechanical sounds. This was different and they were petrified. No sign of Rudi or *Onkel* Schoh.

Abruptly the sounds stopped. Dead silence.

Trudi finishes the story. "Then we heard a loud knock on our basement door and Rudi called out, 'Open up. Come out with your hands up and walk very slowly. The war's over for us. The Americans are here.'

"We had been liberated, yet I was still incredibly frightened. We children had been taught that Americans were monsters with horns and fang teeth. Was I going to see these monsters when I left the basement and climbed out of the rubble with my hands up?

"Outside, I saw big tanks on the street and not a soul in sight. I whispered to Rudi, 'Where are they?' Rudi said calmly, 'Just keep walking. Go slowly and look over the picket fence.'

"The soldiers were lying down, resting near the tanks. Standing on my tiptoes, I peeked over the fence and saw my first American. He wore a helmet and had a round, friendly, clean-shaven face—a handsome fellow. He looked up and smiled at me, showing off a mouthful of beautiful white teeth. Where are the fangs? I thought.

"He reached into his pocket and gave me a gift—a shiny green package of thin sticks. My first chewing gum."

Germany surrendered to the Allies on May 7, 1945.

Later in the day, the American soldiers arrived in force. They wheeled a cannon into the parlor of Trudi's wounded house and positioned it so the cannon's barrel poked out through the huge bomb hole. Other soldiers searched each house for Nazis and weapons.

During the hunt, the villagers moved to tents in the woods. After a short time, the Americans allowed Trudi and her family back into their basement as a reward for her *Tante* Hedwig's role in saving a French prisoner's life by hiding him in her basement.

A day later, Trudi saw German soldiers trudging through the woods with their hands up, prisoners of the Americans—such a sad sight to her.

Once the Americans were organized, they pitched tents in the woods and allowed the rest of the villagers to return to their homes. When the village ladies were asked if they would do the

Trudi and her friend, Alma

soldiers' laundry, Anna volunteered, recruiting Trudi to carry the clean laundry back to the American camp.

The soldiers made friends with the children by giving them chocolate, candy bars and chewing gum. Trudi thoroughly enjoyed chewing each piece of gum until the taste was gone; then she swallowed it. She comments, "I had never lived so well in all my life. For the first time since the war began, my tummy was full of sweets."

Their house was commandeered to house soldiers, who lived upstairs while Trudi's family continued to live in the basement. The house also became a warehouse for Army provisions stored in the kitchen, dining room and sheds. A friendly American soldier was stationed at the house to guard the food. Deciding that Rudi and Trudi were too skinny, he brought Anna a big five-gallon metal can of peanut butter. After opening the can and sticking a spoon in it, he placed the can on a chair by the basement door. The soldier told Anna every time either Rudi or Trudi went by, she should give them a spoonful of peanut butter to fatten them up.

Cooking oil! was Anna's first thought, as she saw all the oil floating on top of the peanut butter. She eagerly scooped it up and saved it. Each day she removed more oil as it rose to the top. The natural peanut butter became denser and denser, more and more like cement, but Anna still made sure to stuff it into her children's mouths at every opportunity. Soon Trudi hated peanut butter, though she loved the candy and gum she ate every day.

The villagers were now forced to share their town with strangers who dictated change. Even drinking water was affected. Fearing the groundwater was polluted, the soldiers ordered the villagers not to drink any water unless it was boiled first. One day, Trudi, alone in the house and thirsty, looked for milk or her mother's homemade *Saft* (juice) made from rhubarb, cherries or raspberries, but found nothing. Desperate, she thought of the *Most* (new wine) in the basement. Every fall *Onkel* Schoh used apples and pears to make *Most*, processing them in the basement winepress and fermenting the liquid in oak barrels. When Trudi's family drank *Most*, they allowed her to have small portions.

In the basement, Trudi filled a big, brown, glazed pitcher from the barrel. After drinking the entire pitcher, she went outside to play. All of a sudden her legs began to buckle. She leaned against the picket fence and slid down to the ground, wondering what was wrong. Anna found her and quickly realized Trudi was drunk. Without a cross word, she gently helped Trudi into the house for a long nap.

Homemade Juice

Use Concord grapes, rhubarb, currants, raspberries, strawberries or cherries.

1. Place the washed fruit (stems, pits and all) in the basket of a steam juice extractor and steam for forty-five minutes.

2. Open the tubing, and the juice will flow out.

3. Freeze, can or drink it fresh. To can the juice, add $^1/_2$ c. of sugar per quart jar.

4. Add sugar or water to taste before drinking it.

The juice can also be used to make jelly.

Trudi's steam juice extractor is one of her favorite kitchen tools. She cannot imagine living without it, although it's not as popular in this country as it is in Europe. Steam juice extractors are found in specialty catalogs. See the appendix for information about one source.

When the Americans discovered the wealthy owners of the closed restaurant (now a warehouse) had been hoarding food, they encouraged everyone in the village to help themselves. Enthusiastic villagers pushed their way into the warehouse to grab as much food as they could carry. Trudi tagged along with Rudi and wandered around, not knowing what to take. Someone handed her a big square box and said, "Take this home." After struggling all the way home with the heavy container, Trudi proudly presented it to her excited mother. Anna's face fell when she pulled out envelopes of ochre powder, a floor stain.

The Americans quickly converted the warehouse into a dance hall. Although no children were allowed inside, Trudi loved listening to the big band music. One evening, her curiosity led her to climb through a window and watch handsome American soldiers with crew cuts twirling pretty girls around the dance floor.

Just as Trudi tried to escape out the window, an American M.P. caught her and asked, "What are you doing, little girl?"

She tried to look innocent and answered with the few words that she knew, "I? No." With a smile, he let her go.

Everyone in the village wondered about the Americans. To Trudi, they seemed like fascinating beings from another planet. What were they eating? What were they reading? She dug through the soldiers' garbage cans, full of new scents and interesting wrappings. Comic strips were fun to find, but most prized of all were thick Sears and Roebuck catalogs that became her favorite reading material. As Trudi puzzled out the words in the product descriptions, she expanded her English vocabulary.

Hearing an English conversation one afternoon, Trudi hid behind a big tree to watch two soldiers tossing a bright orange ball back and forth. When one soldier dropped the ball, it rolled down an embankment into the tall grass. Unable to find it, they finally gave up and walked away. Determined to play with that ball, Trudi began combing through the grasses and scouring that gully. After searching for what seemed like hours, she finally found it. The heavy ball had an odd, bumpy texture, and Trudi took it right home to show her mother. Anna peeled it and nine-year-old Trudi ate her first sweet, juicy orange.

※

One day Trudi complained about a stomachache and her mother scolded her, "Serves you right, *Trudl*, eating all that junk." After three days of increasing pain, Trudi collapsed on the street.

When a neighbor found her and carried her home, Anna suddenly realized it wasn't just an upset stomach but a dire emergency. What could she do? The village had no doctor, but she remembered an infirmary for American soldiers set up at one of the houses. She grabbed Trudi and ran.

The doctor laid Trudi down on a table, felt her stomach, pricked her finger and put the drop of blood in a little box. When he turned to her mother, all Trudi heard was, "Ten minutes."

Sirens went off and the ambulance arrived. Two men grabbed her and practically threw her onto a stretcher. They rushed her into the ambulance so fast they bumped her head on the doorframe. After racing to the hospital, they immediately took Trudi to the operating room. When an ether strainer device was lowered onto her face, she saw a bumblebee buzzing through hundreds of daisies. Told to count to ten, she was asleep after "three."

The doctor had been telling Trudi's mother they had ten minutes to get Trudi into surgery before her appendix ruptured. Although it did rupture during the surgery, the American doctor saved Trudi's life.

After the surgery, many of her new soldier friends came to the hospital to visit, bringing bags of candy. The soldiers who were too busy to visit sent more sweets. Horrified when she saw the piles of candy, Anna said, "No wonder she was sick." The doctor corrected her and explained that Trudi's appendix had been filled with chewing gum. Trudi was given simple instructions after the operation: chew the gum and spit it out.

❧

To celebrate the first Christmas after the war had ended, American soldiers and nurses invited the village children to the former German airfield, Fliegerhorst, for a special party with Christmas presents, ice cream, cake, hot chocolate and the ever-present candy. Such generosity amazed and charmed the children and their families.

Those postwar years, though exciting to the children, were still dangerous. During the war, equipment had been left behind during American-German skirmishes in the woods. Trudi and her friends loved scavenging for war litter, including everything from guns, rifles and bullets to blankets, helmets, shoes and canned Army rations. They carted home the prized blankets, clothes and food. Trudi's mother turned blankets into pants and jackets worn by her children for years.

One day Trudi found a big tin can with numbers, but no label. When Anna opened it, she was elated to find a huge ham and served it for days. A week later, after Trudi found a similar can, her mother invited friends and relatives over for a ham dinner. Anna set the table with her best china and prepared side dishes. Opening the can with a flourish, she discovered not ham, but dried onions. Gales of laughter accompanied dinner that night as they joked about the onions. For years, "Remember the onions" made everyone chuckle.

Many postwar children devised extraordinary, even deadly, toys and games. After the children figured out how to dismantle bullets, they poured the gunpowder out into neat little piles, lining them up so that one acted as a fuse for the next. They lit the first pile and watched the fireworks. Like incendiary dominoes, each pile exploded with a sizzle.

In 1946, Trudi was ten when the lighthearted fun turned deadly. Five friends from a neighboring village found an unexploded hand grenade in the bushes and decided to play soldier. They climbed up the sledding hill on the way to the farms and threw the grenade down to the road, twenty feet below. It detonated, sending deadly shrapnel through the air, killing one of her friends and badly wounding the others.

To cope with her overwhelming sadness, Trudi once again buried it deep inside.

❦

Her *Tante* Liesel's incredible story was a welcome distraction. A war widow, she lived in a small apartment in Feudenheim, twelve kilometers away, and routinely rode her bike five kilometers to her rented city-dweller's garden plot. Trudi loved to visit the tiny, one-room garden house, with just enough room for a woodstove, bed, table and a few chairs.

Back in the summer of 1944, Liesel had begun to notice that vegetables were disappearing from her garden. She asked her family if they had taken any of her produce; of course, they hadn't. When she discovered things in the wrong place in her garden house, she realized someone was living there. After leaving a note warning the intruder that she was ready to call the police, she found a reply tacked to the door. "Come to the *Bierhaus* in Mannheim tomorrow at noon."

When Liesel entered the dimly lit pub, she saw an old man with raggedy clothes and a long beard hunched over a back table, a battered cane propped against the wall near him. She was about to leave when he beckoned to her. Cautiously she approached him. "*Ich bin der Willi,*" he whispered.

It was her husband, Willi. She almost fainted with shock. He had been the one living in the garden house and eating her vegetables! He explained what had happened. After the Russians attacked, everyone else in his German Army unit was killed. Willi saved his own life by diving into the swamp, holding his breath underwater and then breathing through a reed—until he felt safe.

Thirty-six-year-old Willi survived in the swamp for six months, using his naturalist's knowledge to hunt for food and build a shelter. He disguised himself as an old man by growing a long beard, using a pillow as a hump in his back and leaning on a cane. Then he began the seemingly impossible journey of 1,100 miles home from the Russian front. Traveling mainly at night, he lived off the land, eating wild mushrooms and berries and stealing food when possible.

Liesel then hid Willi in their apartment for the rest of the war. She confided in Elise who helped out by bringing them food, but no one else in the family knew about Willi, not even his parents. While in hiding, Willi passed the time by fingering all his favorite accordion tunes without making a sound; he couldn't risk being discovered by the Nazis.

Even after liberation, if Willi were found without Army discharge papers, he would be sent to prison. One morning Liesel heard American soldiers stomping up the stairs and quickly stuffed Willi into a small cabinet. While they searched the apartment, she played with her dachshund in front of the cabinet. The Americans never found him, but Willi became so upset he insisted on leaving town. After dark, they traveled to a safe haven, Liesel's parents' house in the country.

Finally Willi couldn't stand hiding any longer and turned himself in to the Americans. Hearing another unbelievable story from a German without discharge papers, they put him in jail while they looked for evidence that he was a Nazi or a criminal. Eventually, however, they released him when they found nothing incriminating.

In 1947, American Quakers arrived and began to feed the schoolchildren with funds from the Marshall Plan, a United States initiative to support the economic recovery of war-torn Europe. Reducing hunger, especially for children, was one of their missions. Eleven-year-old Trudi could hardly concentrate in school as she waited impatiently for lunch. Standing in line with her little enamel pail, she sniffed the air, trying to figure out what yummy thing they would be serving. Once Trudi's pail was filled with a special American taste treat, she was blissfully happy.

The ladies ladled out scrumptious soups, stews and even fancy oatmeal. For breakfast at home, Trudi usually ate unsweetened oatmeal with salt; now, for the first time, she tried oatmeal with raisins, a real delight except for the little husks. Biting down on them, the children spit them out—sometimes on the floor, but mostly at each other. They coined a new name for the husk-laden oatmeal, "spit soup."

Touched by the Americans' kindness and generosity, Trudi's curiosity about their country grew, though it never occurred to her that someday she might actually live there.

GARDEN TIP

Bell collection on large iron pergola

Surprises and Hiding Places

Whether a garden is large or small, make it exciting. It will appear larger if not everything is seen at once. Try a hidden bench or a creative container tucked beyond a tall shrub.

To avoid a large garden bed running on with nothing special to catch the eye, add a surprise—like a berm to create elevation or an unusual conifer cleverly pruned. Create height with a planter, trellis or a solitary tall specimen plant.

Trudi uses hardscape throughout her garden: a boulder grouping, three to five birdbaths placed together, tall planters set among low plantings, pieces of old fencing and statuary. She adores pergolas; like doors in a house, they invite curiosity, enticing you to see what's hiding on the other side. They can also be used as trellises for climbing plants or places to hang bells or wind chimes.

The think tank garden

Gene's bench

Collection of shade-loving plants

CHAPTER FOUR

The Stranger

Double Flowering Hibiscus
(*H. rosa-sinensis*)

For years after the war, a German radio program broadcast the names of people searching desperately for family and friends. Everyone listening felt heartbroken at the endless list.

Even though Anna must have agonized in private about Emil's fate, she remained cheerful—optimistic he would return home. She often told her children, "Your father will come back."

Trudi barely remembered him.

❧

Anna had to struggle with rampant inflation and a devalued, practically useless *Reichsmark*. In addition to the farm's crops, she produced and bartered with poppy seed oil for scarce goods. Two of Trudi's gentle uncles, Willi and Jacob, were desperate enough to become freight train robbers to make ends meet. They once stole cartons of yarn from a boxcar and then found a woman with a knitting machine. They offered her yarn in exchange for her knitting skills. She produced underwear, used for bartering. That Christmas, everyone in the family received silky, knit underwear as gifts.

Despite the hard times, each year Anna made Trudi's birthday special. After bartering for a giant Swiss chocolate bar at the black market in Lampertheim, she took Trudi on the trolley to Heidelberg. As they walked through town up the long hill to the castle, Anna opened her purse and handed Trudi the chocolate, allowing her to eat the entire bar. Even more than the chocolate, however, Trudi savored their special time together.

❧

One day in 1947, soon after her eleventh birthday, Trudi was delivering clean shirts to an American soldier's tent in the woods. Hearing leaves rustle behind her, she turned and saw two strange men running from one tree to another. Were they trying to hide? Who were they? she wondered briefly.

Returning home, Trudi stopped at the front door, alarmed to hear men speaking inside. Her mother never had male guests. Cautiously, she opened the door and peeked inside. A thin, haggard man sat at the kitchen table. His matted, blond hair straggled down his neck, and his faded grey pants and shirt were stained and torn.

Her beaming mother said to her, "*Trudl*, come meet your father."

Trudi confides, "I was shocked and instantly disliked this stranger. I hadn't seen him since I was six. Mama, Rudi and I were buddies, and then this new person showed up and spoiled everything. He was an intruder in my life. I was not happy that he had reappeared, even though he started taking care of us immediately."

He was an intruder in my life.

With vehicles so scarce in postwar Germany, Emil's first task was to dig up and reassemble the parts of their three-wheeled truck, which the family continued to drive for years. Then he bought a cow to provide fresh milk. Next he began teaching Rudi and Trudi to work hard and not complain. "We have twenty-four hours a day, right?" he asked. "I'll give us eight hours to sleep. Isn't that a lot?" They agreed. "Then we work for eight hours. Isn't that normal?" They nodded their heads. "Now we have another eight hours. What are we going to do?"

"What, Papa?"

"We're going to have some fun."

Emil was a tough but fair taskmaster. The children ended up working sixteen hours, more or less, because their father turned work into fun, while also making it fun to work. In the fall, he made digging up potatoes such a special time that it became their family's favorite crop to harvest. After they gathered all the dried potato tops into one big pile, he said, "At the end, we'll have a giant bonfire. Now let's see who can find the biggest potato."

Working furiously all day, Trudi, Rudi, Anna, Elise and Schoh took up the challenge to dig up that prized potato. Trudi smiles as she recalls those potato harvest days. "Someone shouted, 'I've got the biggest,' and everyone ran to see it. Then we all tried to top that with our own 'biggest.' After lots of laughter and heated exchanges over the best potato, the largest ones were placed under the pile of vines and my father lit the fire. We told stories as we waited for the potatoes to cook. When the fire was a pile of ashes, we found long sticks to fish out the potatoes.

"Everyone argued good-naturedly over which potato was theirs until we were each satisfied with our own blackened potato. Then our reward for that long day of work was the delectable inside— food fit to feed the gods."

Inside the house, the family's hard work continued. Trudi loved Saturdays, the day to "make beauty" preparing for Sunday, the day of rest. The whole house was thoroughly cleaned, kitchen first. Its wooden floor was scrubbed with steel wool, waxed and buffed. Using the parlor stove for heat, they cleaned out the woodstove in the kitchen. Once odds and ends were in their proper places, the table was dressed with the Sunday cloth. When her mother was satisfied that all tasks were done, she asked Trudi to go to the garden and cut flowers for the dining room vase.

Trudi loved that clean little house on Saturdays and, ever since then, creating beauty has been a top priority in her life.

Coal shovel centerpiece with Chicken Gizzard
(*Iresine herbstii* 'Aureo-reticulata')

Despite the good times, as Trudi's father regained his health, he became more and more scary to her. Rudi and her *Onkel* Schoh had similar gentle, quiet temperaments; she wasn't used to having a powerful, domineering man around the house. Her father was in charge and laid down the rules; many restricted her freedom. Trudi wasn't ever allowed to be disrespectful and learned to bury all her anger. Unable to argue openly with her father, she opposed him in her heart.

Her daily chores at the house included feeding the chickens and the rooster. They lived in a chicken coop surrounded by a wire fence. Inside the fence, one tall tree shaded the yard. Trudi made her job fun by teasing the strutting rooster. Using a long, straight stick, she poked at the rooster through the fence to make him mad. She was so successful in making him a permanent enemy that eventually she couldn't enter the chicken coop without the stick.

One day the rooster was missing. She looked for him, but he was nowhere in sight. No fun today, she thought as she threw the stick down. After feeding the chickens, Trudi walked toward the gate and suddenly heard a whirr of wings. The rooster, who had been hiding in the tree, flew down and landed heavily on her shoulder. His claws dug into Trudi's flesh as he pecked at her face. She jumped and screamed, but the rooster wouldn't let go or stop his horrible, painful pecking.

Running out of the house, her father yelled, *"Trudl! Trudl!"* When he saw blood pouring down her face, Emil grabbed the rooster's feet. With one violent swing against the corner of the chicken coop, the rooster's head flew off.

They had rooster stew for dinner that night, and Trudi savored every bite.

Emil worked at the American compound, overseeing the heating systems. He loved being in charge, monitoring both the instruments and the men who were shoveling coal. At night he'd sneak back into the compound to steal gasoline. The Americans stood around a blazing fire, smoking cigarettes and guarding the trucks. Blinded by staring into the flames, they couldn't even see the trucks right next to them. After using a little hose to siphon the gasoline, Emil bartered with it on the black market for coal, cement and other necessities.

This stealing seems anomalous for a highly moral man like Emil, although Trudi can explain her father's behavior. "In some cultures, if you steal food because you're starving, you can't be prosecuted. In Germany, this concept is called *Mundraub*, translated literally as 'mouth thievery.' My father lived by that philosophy. He wasn't stealing for profit; he was stealing to take care of his family. My father was an idealist, always for the other person. He never turned away anyone in need. I remember a ragged beggar coming to him and asking to work a day for food. My father looked down at the beggar's bare feet and thought, This fella is older than I am; he needs my socks and shoes more than I do. That day my father worked at the farm all day, barefoot."

> ... he was stealing to take care of his family.

Emil was heavily involved in underground trade until June 1948. Overnight, the new currency base in Germany abruptly shut down the black market. Each family was allowed to exchange up to six hundred old *Reichsmarks,* one to one, for new *Deutschmarks* (about $150 dollars). For any marks over six hundred, they received only one new *Deutschmarks* for ten old marks. But few people, including Trudi's family, had stashed money because of the runaway inflation. Everyone wanted goods.

Once the money stabilized, Emil called a family council and declared, "Now it's worth working extra hard because when we sell something, we can get real money for it." With the cash from the sale of farm products, he made his own bricks and built a little store. Knowing the villagers longed for treats, Emil and Anna decided to make ice cream. They surmised that after everyone in the village ate their midday Sunday dinner, they would enjoy buying ice cream for dessert.

Trudi's parents advertised the store's grand opening for 2 p.m. the next Sunday. When they opened up the shutters that day, a long line of people eagerly waited, holding their own crystal bowls. In the basement, Emil and Anna cranked the ice cream machine furiously, while upstairs in the store, Rudi and Trudi dished it up as fast as they could. At first, the ice cream balls looked perfectly smooth and round. Later in the afternoon, as the ice cream was rushed upstairs faster and faster, it became softer and softer. The excited villagers didn't care.

The Art of the Deal

Trudi learned the art of the deal at an early age. She began by finding out what people wanted. Whatever the task—collecting nettles for farmers, gathering kindling for the villagers, standing in line for housewives or picking asparagus ferns for bouquets—Trudi was willing to do it. A reliable and thorough worker, Trudi always thanked her customers with a smile after she finished the job.

Her smile grew even bigger when she put the *Pfennige* into her piggybank.

In fact, counting money every few days and watching it grow turned into her favorite thing to do.

After their first wildly successful day, Emil said, "I don't think we can do this again with a hand-cranked machine." He quickly bought an electric ice cream maker.

❧

All the happiness and success Emil created, combined with all the care and love he gave his family, didn't change Trudi's feelings. Jealous of his loving relationship with Anna, Trudi longed to go back to the special closeness she had shared with her mother and Rudi.

Trudi treasured the rare outings alone with her dear mama. When she was twelve, one day they went shopping with their new *Deutschmarks* in downtown Mannheim. Stopping in front of a storefront display, Trudi spied groups of pointed yellow things hanging down from a high shelf. "What are those, Mama?"

"Those are bananas, *Trudl*."

"What's a banana?"

"I'll buy you one and you can see for yourself." After her mother handed her the banana, she walked on. Trudi dawdled behind her, trying to eat it, picking at the tough yellow outside skin with her fingernails. Lagging farther and farther behind, she slowly picked off several inches of outer skin. Anna finally looked back, laughed and said, "Let me show you how to eat it." After she peeled the banana, Trudi was shocked to see how little was left to eat. From the first bite, she instantly loved the banana's unusual taste and texture.

❧

As Germany's social life revived in 1948, bands played and dancing became a favored date activity. Several clever ladies in Blumenau went into business selling nosegay bouquets for men to present to their dates. Busy making the nosegays, the ladies hired youngsters like Trudi to cut asparagus ferns for the bouquets.

Trudi had a special plan for her earnings—a bicycle of her own. Because she didn't have enough money saved, her father agreed to pay half. They drove into Mannheim together and chose a shiny, new red bike for Trudi. As the first child in town to own a new bicycle, Trudi was proud that all her saved coins finally added up to something incredible.

After picking all the asparagus ferns on the roadsides and along the railroad tracks, Trudi couldn't find any more nearby. Since she didn't want to give up this lucrative after-school activity, one day she rode her new bicycle out of town to search for a new source. Eyeing a farmer's asparagus field, Trudi gave in to temptation, quickly cutting some ferns, piling them on her bike and then taking off. This became a routine.

Several weeks later Trudi's favorite teacher, *Herr* Heiser, called her up to his desk. "You are ordered to go to the principal," he told her. Puzzled, she walked down the hall wondering what could be wrong. She was a good student, always obedient, rarely in trouble.

The frowning principal stood Trudi in front of his desk while he waved a piece of paper under her nose. "*Trudl*, I am shocked and disappointed in you," he began sternly. "Farmer Kirsch just stopped by to complain that you have been stealing asparagus ferns from him." Trudi was horrified that the farmer had notified the school. After the principal finished scolding her, she promised never to do anything like that again.

Trudi at thirteen

Back in the classroom, Trudi looked so dejected *Herr* Heiser asked what had happened. After she explained, he said, "*Trudl*, that was a really bad thing to do. But since I like your good business sense, I have the answer for you. You need to go to the farmer and apologize right away. Ask him if he knows of any asparagus fields no longer in commercial use that are about to be plowed under. Then get permission to pick there."

Since she couldn't stand anything hanging over her, that same afternoon Trudi went to Farmer Kirsch and apologized. He was understanding and said, "I'm happy to tell you about a field where you can pick all you want."

To avoid her parents finding out from the school, that night Trudi told them the whole story. Since she had already apologized, they weren't too angry.

❧

For Mother's Day 1949, Trudi was thirteen and wanted to give her mother a special present. White Lilacs and Lilies of the Valley were Anna's two favorite flowers. Trudi knew picking Lilies of the Valley in the forest would be easy, but finding White Lilacs would prove to her mother how much she loved her.

Mr. Keller, a friendly old man down the street, had white Lilac bushes, and Trudi knew his obsession was smoking cigars. They made a deal: in return for two huge cigars, he gave her Lilacs for her mother. Trudi charmed her father out of the cigars. For years they all looked forward to their special Mother's Day deal.

Father's Day was different—a day for the men to get together at the local pub. Trudi doesn't remember ever giving her father anything.

※

Emil had a secret that he didn't share with Trudi until she was forty-eight. If teenage Trudi had known about her father's suffering in a POW camp, her heart might have softened toward him.

At the Russian front in 1943, Emil and his buddy, Oskar, became separated from their unit. Chaos reigned in the freezing winter, and they soon realized the hopelessness of the German cause. They headed away from the front, following the setting sun. One by one, ten other German soldiers crawled out of their foxholes and joined them on their march home.

> Emil had a secret he didn't share with Trudi …

When dawn broke one fateful morning, they stopped briefly and huddled together for warmth. As they whispered to each other, a German officer on his way to the Russian front stepped out of the woods and confronted them. He pulled out his gun and forced the bedraggled group of weary soldiers to march back east.

Emil was furious, knowing the hell of war raged not far away. Joining the millions who had already perished was not an option. As a truck driver, he had not knowingly killed anyone during the war, but he knew what must be done. With a pounding heart, Emil waited for the moment when the officer turned his back. Stealthily removing the pistol hidden in his boot, Emil shot him in the back of the neck, killing him instantly.

Panicked, the group scattered. Oskar and Emil zigzagged through the dark, dense woods, trying desperately to outrun the approaching Russians and any other German officers; but the two foot soldiers were no match for the advancing Russian armored vehicles. The men were captured and transported to a Russian POW camp.

At the makeshift camp, Emil devised a bartering scheme to make prison life more tolerable. First, he discovered a way to break out and return to the camp.[1] Then he gathered possessions from the prisoners, escaped and hiked through the woods to nearby German farmers. As a naturalist, he was totally comfortable in the woods. After exchanging the soldiers' possessions for food, Emil filled his backpack, crept back into the camp and distributed the bounty. He never considered leaving Oskar behind and escaping to freedom alone.

[1] Trudi's father never told her exactly how he managed this.

In the summer of 1945, several months after the Russians won the Battle of Berlin, the prisoners were moved to a camp east of Berlin. Again, Emil set up his bartering business—successful until 1946.

Two lost Russian soldiers stumbled upon Emil in the forest. He knew enough Russian to understand when they said to him, "We'll spare you if you'll get us out of here." The three of them quickly hiked toward camp. Nearing a rutted path, they heard a tank approaching. The two Russians hid Emil behind a rock. When the tank moved on, they called him out, but it was too early. The tank came back and captured all three of them.

I'm going to break out tonight.

Back at camp, Emil was thrown into solitary confinement, in a cell with a single window high up in the wall, and never saw the friendly Russian soldiers again. Oskar knew approximately when Emil was due back with the food. When he didn't arrive, Oskar had a hunch and casually walked over to the solitary confinement area. He whistled their secret signal. Emil whistled back.

Waiting until dark, Oskar crept over to the window. Emil whispered, "I've got to get out of here. I'm not going to wait around until tomorrow morning because by then I may be on a train to Siberia. I'm going to break out tonight. If you want to come with me, be here at 2 a.m. I know how to get out."

At midnight, Emil bribed the guard. At precisely 2 a.m., Oskar showed up and said, "I'm coming with you."

They escaped and made their way home, a journey of more than four hundred miles.

❦

After returning home from the POW camp, Emil suffered from frequent bouts of depression. Today he might be diagnosed with post-traumatic stress disorder; back then he suffered in silence. For several weeks at a time, without any known trigger, he retreated into an emotional, brooding black hole, not speaking to anyone. The jolly man who once sang in a barbershop quartet before the war had disappeared. This family anguish was never discussed with Trudi. Anna learned to cover up her distress at her husband's pain, and Trudi learned to stay out of his way.

To soothe her inner turmoil, thirteen-year-old Trudi found happiness in an enticing garden. The wealthiest family in the village had a bounteous garden with a variety of fruit trees. She especially adored their apricot tree, as apricots were her favorite fruit.

On Sunday mornings Trudi routinely walked two kilometers to the Lutheran church in Schönau. One week she decided to skip church and walk in the woods—something she loved to do. When nobody missed her and her parents weren't told, she started to skip church regularly. Instead, Trudi sneaked into the rich people's garden, saw what was ripe and helped herself.

Trudi explains what happened next. "One Sunday, the apricots were finally ripe—golden pink, plump and bursting with juice. I was in heaven and absolutely stuffed myself. Big mistake! At home, when we sat down for Sunday dinner, I couldn't eat a bite. My father asked, 'How come you're not hungry, *Trudl*?'

"I replied without thinking, 'I ate a lot of apricots this morning.'

"My father was surprised. 'Apricots? Where did you get apricots?'

"Quickly I thought of someone else who had an apricot tree, Mrs. Weiler, a friend of the family. Luckily we didn't see her very often. 'At Mrs. Weiler's house . . . She let me eat some.'

"My father smiled, 'That was very nice of her. You're excused from the table then.'

"My sigh of relief was premature. That night the owner of the fabulous garden stormed over to our house to speak with my father. 'Your daughter is sneaking into my garden and stealing my fruit. She started with strawberries and now has taken too many apricots from my best tree. She is making a real nuisance of herself!' he shouted.

"I had never seen my father so angry as he enunciated, 'Where did you get those apricots?' Before I could say anything, I got a good thrashing on my rear end. Even worse, he made me show my poor bruised rear end to *Tante* Elise and *Onkel* Schoh and tell them what I had done.

"I was sobbing in my room when my father came in and asked me if I knew why I had been punished. I fought back tears and said, 'Because I stole the apricots.'

"He said, 'Oh no, I've done things like that. You were punished because you lied.' He sat down on my bed, rubbing my back as he explained, 'No matter what you do, tell me about it. Then I can come to your aid or advise you. But, if you lie to me, I'm powerless to help you. I must know that my children tell the truth.'

"That taught me a lesson I never forgot."

Trudi's stormy relationship with her father worsened as she grew into a pretty teenager. One Sunday afternoon after she turned fourteen, Trudi headed down the street, on her way to her friend Hildegard's house. A boy rode his bike past her and stopped, waiting for Trudi to catch up to him. They chatted innocently as he walked his bike next to her. Before they had walked half a block, Rudi showed up behind them and ordered Trudi home.

"My overly strict father had seen me walking with a boy," Trudi recalls, "and grounded me, just for that."

Teenage Trudi despised her father's frugality as well as his strictness. Now that her family had some money, she wanted to buy pretty new clothes. Instead, she had to wear her old clothes until they wore out. "You have one Sunday dress. Why do you need another one?" her father inquired after she begged for a new dress. When Trudi bought anything with her hard-earned money, he never failed to ask, "How much did it cost?" When she answered, inevitably he would retort, "That's much too expensive."

Trudi remembers her frustration. "Everything was black or white with him, no shades of grey, no way to compromise. When he saw how angry I became, he turned on the sweetness, but I hadn't recovered from my anger and didn't like his abrupt change of personality. Mama said that we were too much alike. I didn't want to hear it."

Now Trudi realizes how helpless her father must have felt when dealing with a teenager who refused to love or even like him. He tried hard to win her over and many times came close to succeeding. Still Trudi stubbornly refused to give up her anger.

Teenage Trudi could no longer keep her emotions hidden. Peter, her twenty-year-old neighbor, loved to tease her and yank her long blond braids. Trudi hated him for causing her pain. Irritated, she swore she'd get even. One day Trudi saw him leaning back against their picket fence while waiting for the bus. This was her chance. She remembered the extra pickets kept in the shed, so she tiptoed out of the house and ran to find one. Creeping up behind him, she hit him repeatedly with that piece of wood. Hearing the scuffle, Trudi's mother looked out the window and came running out of the house to rescue him.

He never came near Trudi again.

Her temper struck again during the winter of 1951. Trudi felt a need to defend Rudi, even though he was five years older. He was so gentle people sometimes took advantage of him. Ursula, a classmate, tormented Rudi so relentlessly that he finally came home fighting tears. Fiercely devoted to her brother, fourteen-year-old Trudi was infuriated and planned her revenge against nineteen-year-old Ursula.

Several days later, she saw Ursula headed for the skating pond. Trudi went to the marshy area next to the pond and cut a bunch of branches. When the next child skated through the marsh, Trudi hid the branches and said, "Hey, Ursula is over there skating. Would you tell her to come over here? I've got some great news for her."

Ursula quickly skated over and said, "So, what's the good news?" Trudi brought her little bundle of twigs out from behind her back and beat Ursula.

Ursula never bothered Rudi again and became surprisingly cordial to Trudi. Once Rudi was happy, Trudi was satisfied.

❦

Trudi couldn't escape the heartbreak of local tragedies. She was especially close to Rudi's friend, Geo, who taught her to swim and ice skate. After school, he worked in a battery factory that used liquid tar. One terrible day the kettle exploded, covering him with boiling tar, and killed him.

Her good friend, Hansl, died of a brain tumor at age fourteen.

Another friend, swimming in the Rhine River, was badly injured when he was sucked into a riverboat with a paddle wheel.

One dear friend became paralyzed after contracting polio.

Friends were drag racing over the railroad tracks in two cars when a train hit and killed six and badly injured the only survivor.

These repeated bouts of mourning foreshadowed a difficult time for Trudi. The following year, a neighbor noticed Trudi's melancholy expression and sad eyes and commented to her mother. Anna asked Trudi what was wrong, but Trudi couldn't share her deep unhappiness. She drifted through a blur of high school years with no clear direction, forbidden to date or even dance with a boy and constantly at odds with her father.

Marriage seemed the only escape.

The rotunda garden

The dance floor garden

GARDEN TIP

Garden Rooms

From the moment friends and visitors leave the street and walk through Trudi's friendship gate, they are entranced by the textures, shapes and vibrant colors in her garden rooms. Next to the driveway, Trudi's shade garden nestles under a large oak tree. A meandering path leads past an array of woodland plants, including Astilbe, Hostas and Japanese Painted Ferns *(Athyrium nipponicum* 'Pictum'). Bleeding Hearts *(Dicentra spectabilis)*, plants she has loved since childhood, thrive in the dappled shade.

Strolling toward Trudi's backyard, visitors enter her rotunda garden, the only garden room lacking the usual abundance of glorious colors. Instead, Trudi concentrated on creating pleasing green combinations, using foliage of contrasting shapes and textures. Her favorite grass, Hakone Grass *(Hakonechloa macra* 'Aureola'), grows especially well in this shaded area.

Behind the rotunda garden, Trudi designed the dance floor garden, a bluestone patio surrounded by a circle of fragrant plants. She added planters and several benches around the edges of the patio to enhance the design. Forever the romantic, Trudi created the garden as a gift to Bill, wishing they might learn to ballroom dance together. But not even the sweetly scented fragrance garden planted around the dance floor enticed him to try. Can't win them all, Trudi muses.

The sound of gurgling water hastens visitors' steps to Trudi's most ambitious garden room, the pond garden, completed in 1992. She designed a series of pools connected by a small stream and waterfalls. Steve Boese from Hinsbrook Landscaping was her partner in designing and creating the pond, home to Koi fish families, frogs and Water Lilies.

The shade garden

The pond garden

Path leading to the white garden

PART TWO

AMERICA

Steps to the rotunda garden

The Covenant

Asiatic Hybrid Lily *(Lilium* 'Mont Blanc')

Trudi's anger, fueling her desperate desire to escape from home, left her vulnerable. Günther, a family friend and the son of Sandhofen's police chief, began seriously courting Trudi when she was seventeen. When he brought Trudi little presents and took her out for fancy dinners in Mannheim, she was dazzled. She had never met a man as charming and dashing as Günther—tall and suave, with dark, piercing eyes, straight black hair and impeccable clothes. He worked as a detective, spoke four languages and seemed incredibly intelligent.

Trudi knew every girl in town coveted Günther—the prize. Despite the adoring circle of women, he chose her. As soon as she turned eighteen, he proposed. Then, in a rare moment of honesty, he confided a startling truth. He had seen Trudi for the first time when she was only fourteen, selling ice cream in the store. He knew immediately he wanted her and would marry her. Flabbergasted and flattered, Trudi didn't question why a sophisticated twenty-three-year-old man had wanted an innocent fourteen-year-old girl. She immediately accepted his proposal.

Four months later, in the summer of 1954, they were married, with the blessing of Trudi's parents. Since Günther didn't want a fancy event, the official wedding took place at the town hall, with family and friends as witnesses. Following the traditional church service that afternoon, Trudi's parents hosted a small party at home.

Trudi never had a wedding night. Günther was too drunk.

After returning from their honeymoon in Austria, Günther informed Trudi he didn't want any children, ever. Astounded, she questioned him; he turned on her, glaring with such venom that she swallowed her protests. She lay in bed that night praying he'd change his mind. She squelched her next errant thought—could she have made a terrible mistake?

The same thought recurred often as Trudi became isolated from her friends, not even attending her cousin Rosa's wedding. The event wasn't important to Günther and he saw no reason for Trudi to go either. She wasn't allowed to visit with her dear friend, Greta, who lived a block away. When Greta died during pregnancy, Günther refused to let Trudi go to the funeral. Unable to cry, she retreated into her own emotional prison and could barely function.

Günther worked odd, unpredictable hours. He insisted that where he was and what he was doing was none of Trudi's business. She certainly couldn't ever say, "Please be home for dinner at six," yet he insisted she be there when he got home. No matter what time it was, even if he had been away all day and half the night, he expected Trudi to have one of his favorite meals ready. Dutifully, she stopped everything and cooked for him.

Trudi dreaded evenings because Günther drank. Then, the smallest thing made him irate and he could cut Trudi down with just a look. Since he never was staggeringly drunk, it took her a long time to realize he was an alcoholic.

Trudi lived in fear… scared to come home.

Trudi lived in fear. "If I ever went out, I was scared to death to come home. What if I was five minutes late? What if I didn't do something he asked me to do? I was always on the verge of panic. Yet, we never argued, never had a screaming fight. I was too frightened for that. He never hit me, just battered me with words and glares."

Trudi felt like his possession, present only to satisfy his needs. Günther came home to get what he wanted but never was there when she needed him. She never knew how much money he made or where it went. Since she received no money from him, Trudi's income came exclusively from her ice cream store.

On one ordinary Saturday, they strolled into the village bakery and stood in line. While they waited to be served, a rumpled man reeking of beer staggered into the store. For no apparent reason, he picked up a piece of cake and threw it at Trudi. Startled but unhurt, she wiped the icing off her blouse.

Livid, Günther pretended to befriend the man and coaxed him to their apartment. Just inside the door, Günther turned and pulled out his blackjack, always kept hidden up his sleeve. He hit the man over the head. Trudi froze with horror. The man fell to the floor, but Günther dragged him up and hit him in the face. He fell again, blood spurting from his battered nose.

Appalled, Trudi left the room. When she heard the door slam, she went to the window and moved the curtain just enough to see the man, drenched in blood, stumble down the street. Petrified, Trudi expected the police would find a corpse in a few days. Although she had regarded Günther as a frightening menace, that horrible day exposed her husband's dark soul.

As much as she wants to forget those miserable years, Trudi recalls how hard she tried to make their marriage work. She believed that once married, it was her job to stay and make it work. "Divorce wasn't common in the fifties in Germany," she explains.

Trudi's family and friends had no idea of her plight; Günther's charm had bewitched them all. At work, his status remained sacrosanct since he knew about his fellow detectives' illegal activities. Flaunting this control, he swaggered through town, frequenting bars and clubs, and never answered to anyone for anything.

※

For five years of her marriage, Trudi was more miserable than she had ever been during or after the war. With no appetite, she became addicted to Coca-Cola for the energy it gave her to get through the day. She grew extremely thin, ninety-five pounds, despite her 5'7" height.

Unconsciously mirroring her parents' beliefs about privacy, Trudi once again shielded her family by hiding her pain. Even her dear brother Rudi, busy with his own life and career, didn't suspect the truth, and Günther knew enough to avoid him.

Although her childhood faith had been shaken by the hardships of war and the cruelty of her marriage, Trudi pleaded silently for help. She promised to spend her life in service to others if she could only escape from her marriage.

Her plea was answered with an opportunity. In Trudi's family, traditionally the newest car was loaned to vacationers. When Trudi's parents went to Italy, they borrowed Günther's brand-new, grey Volkswagen. The night the car was returned, Günther came home, drunk, and went to examine his precious car. Just minutes later, he stomped into the house, yelling at Trudi. "Your father scratched up my car. I'm going over there right now!" He violently slammed the door on the way out.

> ...Trudi realized that this was her big chance.

Trudi cautiously waited a few minutes before following him. When she reached the front door of her parents' house, she heard the shouting match between her husband and father. For the first time, her father was witnessing Günther's fierce temper. Suddenly filled with a surreal calm, Trudi realized this was her big chance. She stepped into the house and said, "Let me add to this royal shouting match." Turning to Günther, she declared, "I'm leaving you and filing for divorce."

Stunned into silence, Günther and her parents stared at her. Trudi continued, "You've made me miserable for five years. You always put me down; you're never kind or gentle." An unwelcome tear rolled down Trudi's cheek and her voice wavered. "I don't think you ever loved me."

Trudi's father walked over and gently put his arm around her. She straightened. "I never know when you'll be home. You yell at me if your dinner isn't ready and waiting." Out of the corner of her eye, Trudi saw her mother's stark white face. "I have cried myself to sleep more nights than you can imagine. I can't stand living with you anymore. I'm staying with my parents now."

Trudi's father turned to Günther and shouted, "Get out and don't you ever dare come back here!" He forcefully propelled the stunned man out the door.

As the door shut, her father silently gathered her into his arms, and at that moment Trudi had a revelation. Her years of silent anger vanished, like the sky clearing after a ferocious storm. She finally understood what an incredibly loving and supportive father she had.

> Her years of silent anguish vanished…

Trudi emptied her heart to her parents that night and told them she'd rather die than go back to her husband. Several hours later, Günther, spiffed up and sober, knocked on the door and pleaded to speak to Trudi. Emil refused to let him in the house. Trudi stood inside the door and listened as Günther, with his old charm, tried to change her mind. She refused. Emil finally shut the door in his face.

The next day, he phoned and again tried to persuade her. They had the longest conversation of their five-year marriage. Trudi was adamant; she would not go back.

The lawyer hired by Emil questioned Trudi's motives for getting a divorce. He reminded her that under German law, the party who left the marriage was legally to blame. Since she couldn't prove mental cruelty, Trudi had to agree to be the guilty party. This shame was like wearing a scarlet letter "A" on her chest. Trudi agreed in order to free herself from that marriage.

Even Trudi's father, knowing she would never return to Günther, cautioned her about the divorce, "You don't change men the way you change socks." She walked away from him, refusing to dwell on any future consequences.

A few days later, Trudi returned to the apartment to retrieve her things—on a day when she knew Günther was at work. In the bedroom, to make sure she had all her personal property, she checked all the drawers, cabinets and the closet. When she opened his bedside table drawer, she found her salvation—a stack of pictures of women and men in compromising sexual positions, among them Günther and a number of his co-workers. Trudi scooped up the photos and took them straight to her lawyer. With great pleasure, he called her husband, informing him of their leverage and imposing a new settlement. Either he'd confess in court to being the guilty party or the pictures would be made public. Günther, infuriated by his helplessness, was trapped.

Trudi obtained her divorce as an innocent person and never spoke to Günther again.

Crown of Thorns *(Euphorbia milii* 'Valentine'*)*

She now reflects on how those painful years affected her. "Looking back at that terrible time in my life, I was such a fool to stay married for five long years. Yet, I believe people need some suffering in their life to come to their full potential. After I was pushed into survival through the war and a rotten marriage, I learned what was important in life.

"No one has the right to deny you joy."

Bee Balm *(Monarda didyma* 'Cambridge Scarlet'*)*

Invasive Plants

Trudi learned to be selective in choosing garden plants. When groups tour her garden, she often shares stories about how much money and time she wasted in the past by making poor choices at garden centers. Ever so quietly, those sweet-looking little plants exposed their nasty habits. Some spread thousands of tiny seeds into every crevice of her Garden beds, walks and driveway, while others sent aggressive, rhizomatous roots throughout the flower bed.

One January, while traveling, Trudi found a tiny plant that looked interesting. Using a nail file, she carefully dug it out, wrapped it in tissue paper and put it in her traveling soap dish. It survived four weeks of traveling and lived in a pot on her windowsill until spring. After planting it in her garden, she eagerly anticipated each new leaf.

The following year her mystery plant had huge leaves and insignificant flowers on six-foot-tall scapes that constantly flopped over—and it was spreading. She said to herself, "Man, what the heck did I bring home?" After much research, she finally identified it as *Cicerbita macrophylla*. According to the *Random House Book of Perennials*, it "often persists as a roadside weed after it has been thrown out of a nearby garden."

That incident cured Trudi of indiscriminate plant collecting and prompted her to declare war on all invasive plants, no matter how pretty their flowers. Only well-behaved, clumping plants are welcome in her garden. She learns as much as possible about each plant she buys. Plant species new to her are confined to her hidden trial garden for two years. Only if they still please her by being well behaved are they invited to the parlor, her glorious display garden.

The exception to this rule, for Trudi, is Bee Balm *(Monarda didyma)* because of its striking color. Since the plants become too invasive after three years, Trudi moves them after two. In early spring, when new growth is two or three inches high, she removes the sprawled-out plant. Ten to fifteen individual stems are bundled together into one handful and planted in a spot where a splash of midsummer color will be welcome.

View from the fragrance garden to the rotunda garden

Dwarf Astilbe *(A. chinensis* 'Visions')

CHAPTER SIX

A Dream

The five-year nightmare was over. Twenty-three-year-old Trudi was free to regain strength, dream and do everyday things without fear. She loved making others' lives happier. In December, she picked out gifts from her store, including socks, chocolate and stationery. Dressed up like St. Nicholas, Trudi drove around the area, giving presents to friends and strangers alike.

Her parents had given her the ice cream store when she was eighteen. Now Trudi expanded it, selling everything from bread and liquor to books and notions. Other jobs and classes filled her life to the brim. Early in the morning, she worked at her father's cut-flower whole-sale business before opening her own shop for the day. Occasionally she helped out in a friend's dress shop. In addition to taking evening business classes, Trudi studied English and history with a tutor on Saturdays.

After five years of isolation, she relished meeting new people. One fascinating man who traveled the world with his kayak arrived in Blumenau to present a slide show of his adventures. He inspired Trudi to buy her own single-seater kayak to paddle on the Neckar River. Even though he wanted to become more than a friend, the idea of dating petrified Trudi.

When she renewed her friendship with her childhood buddy, Hannelore, her longing for companionship and fun was satisfied. Trudi finally had time for the teenage fun she had missed. Her first indulgence was a new fire-engine-red Volkswagen that took Trudi and Hannelore to all the carnivals and pretzel, wine and beer festivals in the region. They double-dated, swam, and went everywhere as a team. Trudi savored each experience, but refused to dance. She still didn't want to get that close to a man.

After two years, Trudi, without any plan or purpose, realized how shallow her life had become. When Hannelore seriously considered marriage, Trudi felt as though she were drifting into nothingness. The villagers began talking about why she hadn't settled into a second marriage. Even her father grew concerned. After Trudi fixed supper one evening, he commented, "You'll never meet another husband behind the stove." She began to worry he would choose a husband for her.

Poppy Dolls

Since they had few store-bought toys during the war, each spring Trudi turned the field's orange poppies into her doll family. After making five or ten poppy dolls, she pulled reeds from the drainage canal and created furniture for them.

Trudi often parked her car in a field close to the railroad tracks—her place to ponder and dream about the future. Surely this big world had more to offer. Ever since she was a little girl, she had loved tramping through that field and watching the trains go by. The field became her playground. She picked colorful flowers for her mother—dandelions, fragrant spring violets, daisies and other wildflowers—and waved to people on the trains.

Trudi remembers her childish excitement when the train's whistle sounded and the ground began to tremble. Often, when the wartime freight trains rumbled by, the generous conductors would throw down huge chunks of coal. The children would eagerly gather up the splintered coal in little buckets and carts and take it home to heat their houses. If the trains were transporting apples for the troops, instead it rained juicy apples.

As a child, Trudi dreamed that some day one of those trains would take her far away.

※

By the time she turned twenty-six and imagined the future, restless wanderlust dominated Trudi's thoughts. She wanted to see the world and started thinking seriously about leaving Germany, which had begun to feel too confining and familiar. With enough money saved for a year's travel, Trudi decided to turn her dream into reality. The following year, 1963, she planned to travel through North and South America, hoping to reach Buenos Aires, where her mother's cousin played cello in the Buenos Aires National Symphony. Just in case she ran out of money and had to work abroad, Trudi applied for an immigration visa to the United States.

As Trudi made her plans to travel, an American Army pilot, twenty-seven-year-old Captain Bill Temple was given a six-month ground assignment as Operations Officer in Blumenau. On a warm summer day, three weeks before completing his assignment, Bill and his East German friend, Charlie, discussed a place to go swimming. Charlie suggested visiting his friend, Trudi, who knew all the best swimming holes.

While dusting her room that Wednesday evening, Trudi shook the dust cloth out the window. When she heard Charlie calling up to her, she looked down and chuckled to realize she had just shaken the dust cloth out right over their heads. After inviting them upstairs, she met Bill, a handsome man with a short brown crew cut and kind, hazel eyes. Instantly attracted, Trudi peppered Bill with questions about America. As they compared their recent trips to Paris, their animated discussion often excluded Charlie.

Captain Bill Temple, 1962

Before the men left, Bill asked Trudi if he could take her out to dinner. "That would be nice," she replied.

Trudi left the entire weekend free; Bill never called. She stayed home alone, growing more and more annoyed. Finally, on Monday he walked to her house and asked her out to dinner. Trudi said, "No."

Tuesday he again showed up and asked her out. Still aggravated after losing the whole weekend on his account, Trudi said, "No, absolutely not. I'm busy."

On Wednesday he returned once more and asked, "May I please take you out to dinner? This is the last time I'm going to ask you." He seemed so nice that Trudi relented, suggesting they eat at her favorite Chinese restaurant in Mannheim that night.

Although Bill spoke no German, Trudi had been studying English since listening to the BBC in the basement. They ate and talked for hours. She liked hearing about American customs and loved the comfortable feeling of getting to know Bill, without the phony pizzazz she had experienced during her romance with Günther. That first date she told Bill she was divorced, knowing the longer she waited, the harder it would be. Bill's momentary silence told Trudi she had caught him off-guard. Then they easily resumed their conversation.

Luckily, Trudi's parents were on vacation; her father never would have approved of her going out with an American. Reserved and traditional, Emil had developed a fundamental dislike of Americans. He was offended by feet propped on desks, constant gum chewing and loud jazz music. He preferred feet on the floor, a quiet cigarette and a lilting Strauss waltz.

For their second date, Trudi invited Bill to join her American friends on an outing to Heidelberg Castle. Quiet, calm Bill fit in perfectly. After they toured the castle, Bill and Trudi strolled over to the parapet for a view of the Neckar River, sparkling with sunshine and busy with barges and ferries. Bill surprised her by reaching over to hold her hand. When they arrived home that evening, he kissed her lightly on the cheek.

The next day they drove to the Black Forest with German friends. Anna, home from vacation, was aware of Trudi's new admirer. She helped Trudi put together a picnic basket of ham sandwiches, potato salad, pickles and a big jar of strawberries. Anna, unlike Emil, appreciated and liked Americans, since they had helped her survive after the war.

On the way to the picnic site, Bill stepped in a hidden stream and muddied his shoes. There was no explosion, no cursing, no Günther-like response. He simply said, "Oh, shoot," as he bent down to clean his shoes with his handkerchief. Trudi was relieved and impressed by his mild manners.

They spread a flowered tablecloth in a meadow full of daisies, butterflies and summer warmth, enjoying each other's company. When Trudi picked up the strawberries, the bottom of the jar broke, spilling berries and creating a sticky mess. Apprehensive, Trudi looked at Bill, expecting a tirade. Stunned by her look of fear, he hastened to reassure her. They cleaned up the mess together.

On the way home, Trudi couldn't help asking Bill how much longer he was going to be in Germany. Her face fell when he answered, "Only two more weeks." Bill, seeing her sad expression, was elated. She must like him! At Trudi's door, he kissed her gently, then went directly to his commanding officer and asked to be one of the last to leave, instead of the first.

The Colonel responded, "Bill, I'll extend your orders on one condition. You bring her to dinner so I can meet her."

For the special guest, the Colonel included corn-on-the cob for dinner, unaware that in Germany, corn was used exclusively for chicken feed. Trudi didn't comment and copied them eating the corn, which tasted surprisingly good.

Trudi passed the Colonel's test and he extended Bill's tour by four more weeks. They dated nearly every day and conspired with her mother to keep their romance a secret from her father. Each evening after work, Emil had a hot bath and wine with dinner. Anna made sure he had enough wine to go to bed early. Then Bill came over and took Trudi out for a few hours. Even at the age of twenty-six, Trudi still had a midnight curfew imposed by her father.

When Bill left for America, Trudi thought it was over. In the middle of the next night, a messenger knocked on her parents' bedroom window to deliver a telegram. Next morning at breakfast, Trudi's father threw the opened telegram across the table and said, "This came for you in the middle of the night. I didn't think it was important enough to wake you up."

Grabbing it, Trudi quickly left the table and read that Bill had arrived safely in America. Even though Anna must have then told Emil that Trudi had been dating an American, Emil never asked Trudi anything about Bill. Maybe he thought she'd forget the American, far across the ocean.

Trudi might have forgotten Bill, if he hadn't begun writing her long letters once a week. Struggling with her written English, she managed to write back twice a month. Trudi was falling in love, although she knew her father still needed to be won over. When she asked her mother and *Tante* Elise for advice, they suggested introducing him to some outgoing, fun Americans to counteract his bad impressions.

Clematis *(C.* 'Nellie Moser'*)*

Potato Pancakes

4 large potatoes, cut into chunks
1 medium onion, cut into quarters
3 large eggs
1 t. salt
$^1/_2$ t. ground pepper
$^1/_4$ t. ground nutmeg
$^1/_2$ c. fresh parsley, chopped
Vegetable or coconut oil

1. Place potatoes, onions and eggs in food processor. Process until finely shredded. (Make sure that all pieces of potatoes are gone. Work quickly since potatoes will turn brown if left for any length of time.) Pour into large mixing bowl. Mix in salt, pepper, nutmeg and parsley.

2. In large frying pan or on griddle, heat 1–2 T. oil (enough to cover bottom of pan) over high heat until smoking hot. Keep pan hot; do not reduce heat.

3. Spoon potato batter into bottom of pan to make a pancake. Spread out batter to make it thin. Cook 3–4 at a time. Turn when bottom of pancake is golden brown. Remove from pan to plate when both sides are golden.

4. Add 1 T. oil to pan and heat before making each set of pancakes.

Makes about twenty-four pancakes, depending on size.

Serve with applesauce, fruit compote, sour cream or sugar.

This is a social event. Have hungry family or friends waiting around the table. Trudi usually has two or three frying pans going at one time.

Bill wrote to suggest calling the cheerful American librarian at the base. Trudi invited her over for dinner one night, and together they made potato pancakes and applesauce. Although her father couldn't speak much English and the librarian couldn't speak much German, Trudi seated them next to each other. The American visitor relished every bite and said to Emil, "I'm really glad potato pancakes don't have any pits, so you can't count how many I've eaten." When Trudi translated, her father roared with laughter. The librarian was invited back many times.

Several months later, Bill wrote to ask whether he might visit Trudi over Christmas. In a bind since she still hadn't told her father, Trudi again turned to her mother and *Tante* Elise. Anna suggested skiing in the Bavarian Alps where friends owned a *pension* (small hotel).

Delighted with the plan, Bill flew to Germany and they drove Trudi's VW Beetle south. On the way to the *pension*, the softly falling snow that had seemed romantic turned into a blizzard. As they approached Fieberbrunn in southern Germany, a truck suddenly went into a skid and glanced off the driver's side of Trudi's car. Amazingly, no one was injured. After wiring the door shut, they drove the car on to the hotel.

The record-breaking blizzard raged for two days and they were confined inside. After innumerable games of cards, Trudi and Bill finally saw the sun again. However, by then the town was isolated under five feet of drifting snow and the car couldn't be fixed; even skiing was impossible. Helicopters had to airdrop food.

Finally the roads were plowed out enough for them to take an evening walk through town. They strolled past townspeople liberated from their houses, shoveling and chatting with each other. When they stopped to admire the snow sparkling on an intricate wrought-iron gate, Bill turned to Trudi. He put his arms around her and quietly asked, "Would you consider marrying me?"

... a truck suddenly went into a skid...

Trudi succumbed to the romantic moment and said, "Yes."

The next day the engaged couple held hands as they walked through the woods looking for a Christmas tree. Bill climbed a small pine tree and hacked off the top. Back at the *pension*, they put it in a tin can, wrapped a towel around the bottom and hung two newly purchased ornaments. On Christmas Eve, Trudi and Bill drove on the snow-packed roads to the cathedral in Oberammergau for the renowned midnight service.

After Christmas, they traveled back to Blumenau and stopped at the Army PX. Bill bought Trudi a plain gold band. She thanked him, but she was already wondering what she had done. She hardly knew Bill. She silently chastised herself, How could I possibly have gotten engaged without even introducing him to my father?

Bill remained unaware of Trudi's doubts as he happily boarded the plane back to America.

Trudi, with such instant cold feet, would not consider herself engaged. Without breathing a word to her parents, Trudi wrote Bill that she wasn't wearing the ring. He understood and reassured her it was all right.

Bill wanted Trudi to come to America right after Christmas, but she had made plans to emigrate the following June and wanted to stick to that date. Her parents didn't yet know she had received United States immigration papers; they believed Trudi was simply going to tour North and South America.

While Bill waited, he wrote to Trudi every day. Impressed by his devotion, she wrote back every week or two.

❧

When the departure day arrived, her father kissed Trudi and said, "Now go out into the world and show them what I taught you."

> ## How could I possibly have gotten engaged...

Trudi insisted on taking the local train to begin her journey, just as she had imagined so many times. The train would take her to the Netherlands where she'd board *The Statendam*, one of the Holland America Line's smaller ships. Hannelore drove Trudi and her luggage to the train station in the middle of the night. Full of anticipation, Trudi hugged her and eagerly turned toward her future.

As soon as Trudi stepped into the train, she pulled the window down to say good-bye to Hannelore. Her head was still hanging out the window when the conductor blew his whistle and slammed the door shut. The window shot up and hit Trudi on the chin.

Trudi's sleeping compartment was already crowded with five other people who had been traveling from Switzerland. The stale air was thick with smoke. She stepped back and instantly closed the door, knowing she couldn't breathe in that confined space. Trudi asked the conductor for another bed, but the only empty spot was a seat in a coach car. For the rest of the night Trudi sat upright, nursing her bruised chin.

At the Dutch border, the guard asked for Trudi's passport. When she handed it to him, he looked at it and shook his head, "That's not you." He handed it back to her. Trudi stared in disbelief at her mother's picture. She rummaged frantically in her purse and found her own passport. The guard nodded and allowed her to enter the Netherlands.

When the train arrived in Rotterdam, a limousine picked up Trudi. She mailed her mother's passport home at a post office on the way to the ship.

At the ship Trudi had to show her passport again. The security guard looked at Trudi, looked at the passport and repeated the same words, "That's not you." With a sinking heart, Trudi reached for the passport. She had sent the wrong one home! All she could think was, How stupid could I be? Surely I will miss the ship. She hurried to the dock supervisor and explained. He motioned to a second supervisor and, after a lengthy discussion, they narrowed the possibilities to seven post offices. They ran to hire a taxi for her.

She and the driver raced into the first two post offices with no luck. The third post office had her passport, but the clerk said sternly, "We can't give it back to you. It's against the rules." Trudi desperately offered to write the address again to verify her handwriting. The stiff-necked clerk compared the two envelopes and reluctantly gave the original back to her. Finally Trudi was ready to sail.

She arrived back at the dock and dashed up the gangway just as the band finished playing the traditional departure song, *"Muss ich den zum Stadtelle heinaus . . ."* ("Must I now leave this little town . . .") Totally out of breath and with her heart pounding, Trudi looked for her cabin, terribly disappointed at missing the embarkation celebration.

After the ship docked in Northampton, England, Trudi thought, OK, now I can enjoy the sailing festivities in England. Wearing her new white suit, she stood at the rail and watched the passengers coming onboard, as crowds of family and friends waved good-bye from the dock.

Suddenly something hard hit her on the head. A passenger grabbed her and led her down some steps. She asked, "Don't you know what happened to you?"

"No," Trudi replied, mystified. The woman explained that a seagull had just pooped on Trudi's head and all over her outfit. While the kind lady helped wash her hair, Trudi again missed the sailing festivities. As she leaned over the bathroom sink, wet hair dripping in her face, she wondered if she should have stayed home.

The eleven-day voyage began. On the third day at sea, Trudi went with Renate, a young woman from a nearby cabin, to a dance. They enjoyed the merriment until they noticed increasing numbers of people leaving the dance hall. Renate asked Trudi, "What the heck's going on? There's nobody here."

"The ship's really rocking. We must be in a storm."

Careening from one handrail to another, they climbed up the stairs and pushed open the door. Out on the heaving deck, they saw the huge waves of a major Atlantic storm battering the ship. The crew had roped off a large section of the bow to keep the passengers away from the waves crashing onto the slippery deck. Everywhere they looked, green-faced passengers were hanging over the railing.

Trudi aboard ship

Fascinated by the storm, Trudi and Renate went back to their cabins and changed into slacks, jackets and kerchiefs. Back on deck, they clung to the railing until someone got sick right next to them. Trudi felt her stomach heave and ran to her cabin. The rest of the voyage she stayed in bed, miserably seasick. Renate, never sick, visited Trudi, but couldn't comfort her.

Finally, the ship reached the St. Lawrence River and stabilized. Trudi's seasickness stopped instantly.

Trudi's long-anticipated voyage dissuaded her from boarding any boat or ship for years. The next time she went home to Germany, she boarded a plane.

❧

After Bill greeted Trudi at the dock with flowers, they went straight to the hotel, where proper Bill had booked separate rooms. After Trudi freshened up, she met Bill at the pool with her prepared speech. "I told him I couldn't get married. I just couldn't imagine marrying him or anyone else. His calm answer was brilliant. He looked me straight in the eye and said, 'That's all right. We don't have to get married. Let's just stay friends. Just do me one favor? Come meet my family. I still want to introduce you to them.' "

Trudi and Bill had a marvelous time visiting his extended family in Canada. The couple drove from his Aunt Edith's house in Toronto to Waterloo and Windsor, enjoying elegant family dinners and sight-seeing. After two weeks of nonstop togetherness, Trudi knew she was in love.

None of his relatives mentioned anything about a wedding until four days before the wedding date. Trudi didn't expect to get married until Aunt Edith asked, "Don't you think we ought to order some flowers for the wedding?"

Hesitating, Trudi thought fast. Aside from their dates before Bill left Germany, they had spent only three weeks together. Yet, she sensed he was the right man for her. To Aunt Edith, she replied, "Sure, let's go."

After they ordered wedding flowers and returned to the house, Bill asked Trudi, "Where were you? I looked all over for you."

"Aunt Edith and I went to order wedding flowers."

He was astonished. "You mean I'm getting married?"

At the rehearsal dinner, they ate hamburgers, Trudi's favorite American food. For the wedding, she wore a white cocktail dress and pointy white shoes. The sixteen wedding guests included the minister and his wife. All Trudi remembers about the wedding dinner is eating fancy, crustless deviled ham and chicken salad sandwiches made from soft white bread—quite a contrast to the dense, crusty German bread she was used to.

After the service, Bill's Uncle Rhys suggested, "Don't you think you had better call your mom and dad and tell them what you two did?"

Apprehensive about calling home, Trudi was relieved when her mother answered the phone. "Guess what? I just got married," she said.

There was silence. "Best wishes," her mother said. As they talked, Trudi sensed the news wasn't entirely unexpected.

Her father wasn't home.

Despite their disappointment in missing the wedding, Trudi's parents sent a large bouquet of roses that same day. Her mother adored Bill and was happy for her daughter. With no other choice, her father waited to meet his new son-in-law.

Mr. and Mrs. William F. Temple

Hosta *(H. montana* 'Aureomarginata'*)*
Japanese Painted Fern *(Athyrium
nipponicum* 'Pictum'*)*

Hosta *(H.* 'Piedmont Gold'*)*
Blue Spruce *(Picea pungens* 'Montgomery'*)*

Arborvitae *(Thuja occidentalis)*
Hosta *(H.* 'So Sweet'*)*
Lungwort *(Pulmonaria officinalis)*
Bleeding Heart *(Dicentra spectabilis)* foliage

Hakone Grass *(Hakonechloa macra* 'Aureola'*)*
Swiss Chard 'Ruby' *(Beta vulgaris* var. *cicla* 'Ruby'*)*

GARDEN TIP

Foliage First

Flowers are ephemeral and display their beauty for only a short time, but the foliage will be there all season. To decide what plant to buy, Trudi looks closely at the leaves. She explains, "When a small person stands next to a tall person, their differences are emphasized. The same principle holds true in the plant world. Plants contrasting in size, color and texture are important to create impact. Think of foliage first."

Chicken Gizzard *(Iresine herbstii* 'Aureo-reticulata'*)*
Broom *(Cytisus supinus)*

Hosta *(H.* 'So Sweet'*)*
Red Barrenwort *(Epimedium x rubrum)*

Sedum *(S.* 'Vera Jameson'*)*
Nippon Daisy *(Chrysanthemum nipponicum)* foliage
Clematis *(C.* 'Henryi'*)* in bud

Fuchsia *(F. triphylla* 'Gartenmeister Bonstedt'*)*
Japanese Anemone *(Anemone hupehensis* 'September Charm'*)*
Ornamental Onion *(Allium christophii)*
Bigroot Geranium *(Geranium macrorrhizum* 'Spessart'*)*
Fountain Grass *(Pennisetum alopecuroides)*

Water Lilies in the pond

Roots

Hosta *(H. 'Piedmont Gold')*

Bill expected Trudi would be content as a housewife—he didn't know her very well.

Their marriage began quietly enough. Trudi was in love, busy fixing up their apartment, knitting and cooking, while Bill completed his last month of active duty service at Fort Lewis, Washington. When he was home, they continued their honeymoon and all was well. But when Bill left on maneuvers for two weeks, Trudi was lost. Leaving all that was dear to her in Germany—family, friends and belongings—was heart-wrenching. In America, everything was new—the food, the shopping, the traffic, the customs. And, for some reason, Trudi wasn't sleeping well. Without a job or purpose, she felt unsettled and frustrated.

In October 1963, they moved to Denver, and Bill began flight training to become a United Airlines pilot. With an income of $350 a month, they lived in a sixty-dollar-a-month basement apartment with a Murphy bed in the wall and a tin shower.

On the third day of flight school, Bill came home to find Trudi exuberant. She had applied for a job as a florist's assistant, banking on her experience arranging her garden flowers in Germany. Hired for $1.25 an hour, Trudi was overjoyed to be busy again.

Newlyweds rarely have smooth sailing; Bill and Trudi were no exception. Their first conflict arose when Bill complained about Trudi's habit of setting the alarm clock to awaken her in the middle of the night. The quiet of the night was her favorite time for thinking, reading, studying and relaxing—without the phone ringing or any other interruptions.

Trudi solved this problem by drinking a large glass of water before bedtime. When she woke up several hours later, she slipped from their bed and luxuriated in the solitude.

Their financial conflicts weren't so easily solved. Bill and Trudi decided they wouldn't buy anything beyond the basics without both agreeing to the purchase. This fiscal policy worked until Trudi found an enticing, multicolored Mexican poncho she absolutely had to have. Bill disliked it and refused to okay the purchase. Trudi was not happy.

In November, Trudi and Bill disagreed again over a four-foot-tall, filigreed brass candlestick. Perfect for our tiny living area, Trudi thought. Again Bill voted no. After cashing her first

Be Frugal

Trudi takes great satisfaction in being frugal without being cheap. Newly married, with little money to spend, she remembered her mother's thrifty ways and then added more of her own ideas over the years.

Today, still trying to "beat the system" and save money, Trudi saves 10%–20% with careful shopping at the grocery store. "What bank," she asks, "gives a better rate of return?" One chicken, stuffed and baked, is used for four meals: stuffed chicken, chicken and stuffing sandwiches and two meals of hearty chicken soup.

Most people don't think twice about throwing out the water after they cook vegetables or potatoes. Not Trudi. She heats that vitamin-rich water to make her own vegetable tea. "Nothing better on a cold winter's day," she says.

Small savings add up. Trudi prefers the more scenic back roads to tollways. During the winter she wears a sweater and wool socks, keeping her house at 58° unless company is coming. Trudi also makes gifts of plants from her garden or food she's prepared.

paycheck, Trudi went back to the store to buy the unique candlestick. It was gone. Disappointed, Trudi asked the saleslady, "Who bought that candlestick?"

"A really nice gentleman."

Although Bill never mentioned it, Trudi often thought about the candlestick episode. Then, on Christmas morning, there was her candlestick, a gift from Bill, the "really nice gentleman." Trudi was delighted by his thoughtfulness, though she still wondered who gave Bill the authority to decide whether she could have something or not?

❧

Often in a marriage, words aren't necessary to convey displeasure. Money was tight for Trudi and Bill. Determined to use only half her weekly food budget, Trudi planned to save the rest. Since she loved adventurous eating, she read and studied about edible wild plants. In the first spring of their marriage, Trudi decided to make "spinach" from Violet leaves. After collecting a large bunch of leaves, she cooked and served them for dinner.

Bill started eating, then abruptly stopped. He pushed his fork into the greens and held it up. "What's this?" he asked.

"It's spinach."

"This is the weirdest spinach I've ever eaten. Come on, Trudi. What is it?"

"They're Violet leaves," she confessed. "The price is right."

A conservative meat-and-potatoes man, Bill looked at her, shook his head and ate the "spinach" reluctantly.

❧

Trudi's father had still not met Bill, although Trudi and Bill had been married for six months. International phone calls were reserved for dire emergencies in the sixties, so her mother wrote letters to the newlyweds. One note made Trudi cry. Her father, probably feeling like his precious daughter had immigrated to the moon, had given all her furniture to Rudi for his vacation home in Austria. Hurt and upset, Trudi vowed to make her own decisions in the future.

In early March 1964, Bill finished flight training and received his United Airlines assignment. He would be a flight engineer, based at Chicago's O'Hare Airport. As Trudi and Bill drove their cars east, the majestic Rocky Mountains slowly disappeared in their rearview mirrors. Trudi fell in love with the prairie vistas as they drove through Nebraska, Iowa and into Illinois. Fantastic, she thought over and over, marveling at America's vastness. When they exited the toll road west of Chicago, Trudi felt a surge of melancholy; the beautiful trip was almost over.

Driving toward downtown Hinsdale, Trudi's sadness disappeared. She signaled Bill to stop. He pulled over and asked, "What's going on? Are you hungry?"

"Yes, that too. But what I would really like you to know is that this is the town I want to live in."

Bill knew Trudi wasn't joking as he gazed at the majestic old trees shading the tranquil neighborhood and the grand houses with their European ambience. "Hmm, I don't think we can afford this," he commented.

He did agree to have lunch in the lovely town. Over sandwiches, Trudi cajoled him into calling a realtor—just for a little information. Later that day, the realtor pointed out a large, two-story Tudor house with an acre of land. Trudi instantly imagined flower boxes under each of the windows, just like many of the houses in Germany. She said enthusiastically, "This is exactly what I would like."

… she knew it was meant to be theirs.

Bill was speechless, and then relieved when the realtor said, "Well, that one's not for sale. I just wanted to know what style house you like."

None of the houses they saw that day were just right, so Trudi and Bill moved into a little studio apartment near the airport and continued their house hunting.

Just before Easter 1964, after weeks of looking, the realtor called. She asked if Trudi remembered the Tudor house that wasn't for sale. She remembered it well, since she had been comparing every house to that one. When the realtor told her the house had just come on the market, Trudi eagerly responded. "We'll buy it. Don't show it to anyone else." Not caring what it looked like on the inside, she knew it was meant to be theirs.

As soon as Bill came home from a trip, they went to see the house. After whisking through it, they agreed it was too large, too expensive and too overwhelming for two newlyweds. They bought it anyway.

The bank dampened their enthusiasm, informing Bill and Trudi they'd have to make a 50% down payment to qualify for a loan. They managed to scrape together the money and slept on the floor for a few weeks until Bill's bachelor furniture arrived.

Trudi eagerly began gardening in her new yard. She watched for the abundant rhubarb the previous owner had told her to expect. What a disappointment when the rhubarb turned out to be Burdock *(Arctium minus)*, an invasive weed that had spread throughout the garden. Undaunted, she dug it up and planted real rhubarb, along with many other vegetables, in their new backyard garden.

Captain Bill

With all the house expenses, Trudi and Bill couldn't afford to furnish the whole house or buy decorative plants for the outside. Generous neighbors and new friends shared their plants with Trudi, who returned the favor as her garden grew. Remembering the German front-yard gardens, she began her flower garden the same way, by planting a small, two-foot border hugging the horseshoe-shaped driveway.

Soon after their first anniversary, Bill gave up his concept of being married to a traditional house-wife. He liked being married to the real Trudi, even when her temper flared. One morning she became angry while making pancakes. Who knows why? Perhaps the pancakes were too thick or too dark. Trudi does remember her reaction. Grabbing the pan, she threw it and the pancakes up in the air, hitting the ceiling. Bill remained calm and quietly said to her, "You had better go for a walk." Trudi stomped around the house a few times before she realized how silly she'd been. Although she apologized to Bill, the ugly grease spot on the ceiling reproached her every time she walked into the kitchen.

Bill knew Trudi still struggled with homesickness and adjusting to her new country. He wondered how to make her life easier. If only Trudi could sleep better, he thought.

❧

During the holiday season that year, Trudi worked in the Sears catalog department taking phone orders. To counteract the monotonous work, each day she challenged herself to beat her own record of orders. At work and around town, she couldn't help disliking the commercial symbols of an American Christmas: flashing lights, artificial trees, tinny holiday music blaring in stores for months. Trudi wished for the simple German Christmas of her childhood.

"For the first day of Advent, my mother tied fresh pine boughs into a wreath, attached four candles and hung the wreath from the ceiling above the dinner table. The pine scent filled the room. We lit one more candle each Sunday until finally it was Christmas.

"Saint Nicholas' Day was the 6th of December. Christmas Eve presents were from the Christ Child. As children, we thought they were from this angel, Jesus Christ, whom we pictured as a beautiful imaginary being who came down from heaven to give us presents.

"Holiday celebrations lasted three days. The stores closed at noon on Christmas Eve and didn't reopen until December 27. On Christmas Eve morning, the adults went out to the woods and cut their own trees. In the early afternoon, we were bathed and dressed in our finest clothes, but not allowed in the parlor. At dinnertime, finally the parlor door was opened and we had our first glimpse of the fabulous tree, glowing with real candles.

"For dinner we had a very special treat, Russian eggs. Actually it has nothing to do with Russia. A large platter was piled with potato salad. Other foods were artistically arranged on top—chicken, lox, deviled eggs, beef, pork and vegetables. Rye bread was always served. That was our Christmas Eve dinner.

"After dinner, we sang songs and opened presents—one from my mother and father and one from *Tante* Elise and *Onkel* Schoh. Because we loved playing all kinds of games and cards, there was always a new game on Christmas. At midnight we went to church whenever possible. For many years we didn't have a church in our village and had to walk to the Sandhofen church. During the war, we couldn't go at all because of the unpredictable bombing.

…Trudi opened a festive box to find…

"On the 25th, we had Christmas dinner for the entire extended family—a big feast of goose with potatoes and vegetables. After dinner we played games, opened more presents and told stories. On December 26, we celebrated with another feast—lots of leftovers and new dishes. The party continued as friends and family visited.

"Christmas was truly something to look forward to."

❧

Trudi and Bill's first Christmas as homeowners should have been a happy one, but Trudi was grumpy. They were alone in their new house—without family or close friends. To make matters worse, Bill gave Trudi the most infamous present of their marriage. With little money to spend on gifts, they agreed to give each other only one practical gift. With great anticipation, Trudi opened a festive box to find six pairs of Sears underpants. Flabbergasted, she turned to Bill, "How could you?" She thought, Honest to Pete, how romantic are cotton panties?

Tante Elise's German Potato Salad

5 pounds potatoes
$1/4$ cup vegetable oil
6 chicken bouillon cubes
1 cup diced dill pickle spears
$1/4$ cup of pickle juice
2 t. salt
1 t. ground pepper
$1/8$ cup fresh lemon juice

1. Place unpeeled whole potatoes in boiling water and cook until soft. Drain, cool and peel.

2. Wait until potatoes are room temperature, but not stiff. Slice potatoes thinly and return to pot.

3. Pour oil over the potatoes. Do not stir. (Make sure that the oil is the first ingredient added to the potatoes.)

4. Dissolve bouillon cubes in 3 cups of boiling water. Add to potato mixture.

5. Add dill pickles, pickle juice, salt, pepper and lemon juice. Mix well and adjust seasonings to your taste.

Holiday Russian Eggs

1. Prepare German potato salad.

2. Prepare any number of the following items, depending on what your family likes. Vary the quantity depending on the number of guests.

   Deviled eggs, using your own recipe

   Chicken drumsticks, seasoned and sautéed in frying pan

   Shrimp, cooked

   Stuffed mushrooms, according to your own recipe

   Cooked asparagus

3. Prepare other ingredients:

   Raw vegetables, such as cauliflower, broccoli and tomatoes

   Leaf lettuce, preferably Bibb

   Slices of deli ham, rolled

   Sausage, cooked and sliced

   Lox, rolled

4. Spoon the potato salad onto a large platter, covering the entire platter. Arrange all the food on top of the potato salad artistically.

Russian Eggs

Mystified, Bill said, "But I know you like that type of panties."

"Not for Christmas!"

By afternoon, the unpleasant odor of sauerbraten roasting in the oven didn't help Trudi's attitude, and she threw it out. Cheerfully, Bill went to the store to buy another roast, this time unmarinated. When the aroma of that roast permeated the house, Trudi again felt ill.

With a quizzical look, Bill asked, "Are you pregnant?"

Trudi burst into tears. "I don't know," she confessed. Bill was thrilled when the test was positive, but Trudi was scared.

❧

In April 1965, Bill was finally eligible for vacation, and they took the long-awaited trip back to Germany for the first meeting between Trudi's husband and her father. Both men, knowing they were now family, made an effort to impress each other. Emil had always loved smiling and immediately approved of Bill's friendly, smiling countenance. Trudi and her father began to bury past tensions and enjoy an adult father-daughter relationship.

> ... Bill finally figured out the mystery...

While in Germany, Bill finally figured out the mystery of Trudi's sleep deprivation. Their American beds were the perpetrators. In Germany, her bed nestled in an alcove with a low ceiling—a cozy cave surrounded by three walls. Back home, Bill immediately bought a new canopy bed with draperies on all sides and solved her problem. At last Trudi could sleep well.

❧

The final step in Trudi's initial adjustment was the fun of creating and expanding her American garden. Even after exchanging plants with her neighbors, Trudi yearned to expand her plant collection. On out-of-town trips, she'd look at people's front yards as she drove by. When she found an intriguing plant, she'd stop, knock on the door and offer the gardener one of her plants in exchange for the one she coveted.

❧

After an uneventful pregnancy and delivery, their daughter, Trudianne, was born in 1965. Bill wanted to buy Trudi a special celebratory present and suggested the diamond ring she hadn't received when they became engaged. Disinterested in jewelry, Trudi asked for a well for her backyard garden. Bill agreed and water became Trudi's perfect birth present.

Trudi had eagerly anticipated her mother's visit, scheduled for a week before the baby's due date. To her great disappointment, her father couldn't overcome his fear of flying and refused to come. Thrilled about being present for the birth of her first grandchild, sixty-one-year-old Anna had made all the necessary preparations, including the required smallpox vaccination, when tragedy struck. Just before her departure date, Anna had a stroke. Six weeks after Trudianne's birth, her *Oma* Anna died in Germany. Rudi later discovered she had received a vaccine overdose.

Of all the sorrows in Trudi's life, this loss was the most difficult to bear.

⁂

In 1969, Trudi and Bill had a second child, Margo. Immediately after coming home from the hospital, Trudi began an old German custom of training Margo to use handkerchiefs as her "lovey." Instead of a pacifier or Trudianne's bedraggled stuffed animal, Trudi had baskets of cotton handkerchiefs for Margo. Easy to hold, the "hankies" became associated with comfort. Because they were so easy to wash or replace, Trudi didn't worry about losing a favorite stuffed animal or pacifier.

From babyhood to adulthood, Trudianne and Margo treasured the special family time when their dad read to them. As the girls matured, Bill adapted his choices—from his favorite, *Where the Sidewalk Ends* by Shel Silverstein, to James Herriot's *All Things Great and Small* series. Even after the girls were grown and out of the house, he continued to read to Trudi.

Even the vegetable garden became fun…

Trudianne and Margo loved to play in their backyard, where an old Box Elder tree supported a rope swing. Its branches bent down to encourage climbing girls to scamper up to the tallest lookout. Near the swing set, the girls peddled their Big Wheels® on an old paved dog run. Even the vegetable garden became fun when the girls competed in corn races—contests to see how fresh the corn could be when they ate it. With the pot boiling on the stove, they dashed out, picked the corn, husked it as they ran back up to the house and popped it into the pot.

Trudi planted a night-blooming evening primrose, an *Oenathera*, in the front garden just for her girls. As the sun set, they'd run home after playing—just in time to watch its flower petals open.

Young Temple Family

Next to a magnolia tree, tall plants surrounded a little island of lawn, creating an invisible oasis when the girls lay down on the grass. Every spring they made poppy dolls in this hideaway, just as their mother had once done in Germany.

Trudianne and Margo had not inherited Bill's aversion to strange foods; they encouraged their mom to make something unusual when their friends came over to eat. They'd run into the house and ask, "Mom, can Susie come over for dinner and will you make something weird?"

Their favorites were wild mushroom chowder, "sumac-ade" and cattail kabobs. Trudi found nonpoisonous mushrooms in the woods to make the chowder. She cut wild sumac to make "sumac-ade" by sloshing the sumac flowers in a bucket of water. The citric acid on the sumac seeds dissolved in the water, turning it pink. Trudi strained the water, chilled it and added sugar. The result—a refreshing pink beverage.

Trudi picked cattails as soon as they came out of the sheath on the plant's stalk, cooked them in boiling water and rolled them in butter; the girls ate them like kabobs. (Though the bottom part of the cattail is not edible, the top part is a delicacy.)

Trudi and Bill were determined to avoid that ultimate parenting hassle: asking their children to pick up their rooms. They decided to set a limit. Instead of saying to their children, "Clean up the kitchen," or "Clean up your room," they asked each girl to pick up fifteen items. Bill and Trudi helped too. Within a few minutes, each of them found fifteen items and was done. This strategy became so successful they could ask Trudianne and Margo to "do fifteen" several times a day. The house was rarely messy.

Trudi used her expanding garden to emphasize the value of hard work and perseverance. Knowing that reaching a goal would give them a sense of accomplishment, she made a rule that her girls each had to pull one hundred weeds a day. Trudianne, testing the system, asked if she could pull two hundred weeds today and none tomorrow. Too smart for that ploy, Trudi insisted on one hundred weeds every day on the honor system.

Each girl had a little bucket and a dull knife. Nothing could stop Margo's concentration as she pulled her quota. Trudianne devised a counting system with ten pebbles; she added one pebble to a pile for every ten weeds she pulled.

The approach succeeded because there was an end to the chore.

To teach the girls not to complain for complaining's sake, Trudi and Bill taught them if they didn't like something, they should "do something about it." Both girls were in the van with Trudi the day they made her follow her own rule. Waiting at a stoplight, they witnessed a person in the car ahead throw a banana peel out the window. Irritated, Trudi said, "Did you see that, girls? What a litterbug!"

Trudianne jumped in. "Mom, go do something about it!"

"All right, I will." Trudi hopped out of the van, as Trudianne and Margo cheered her on. Running up to the car, she picked up the peel and knocked on the window. When the driver rolled it down, Trudi threw the banana peel back into his lap and said, "I think you dropped something." Embarrassed, he didn't say a word. Back in the car, the girls applauded loudly.

As the happy family years passed, Trudi's sleep problems were forgotten. Once in a while, Bill removed one of the fabric panels, until finally they were just a distant memory. Then Trudi came home one day and found her bed perched in the middle of the backyard garden. She asked Bill, "What's going on?"

With a mischievous smile, Bill said. "Go upstairs and look."

Walking into their bedroom, Trudi discovered a gorgeous new king-sized bed, repositioned to view the garden. No four posters, no fabric panels—instead Bill had chosen a style just for her. Trudi traced the intricately carved flowers on the headboard and turned to embrace Bill. The bed, solidly graceful, symbolized the strength of their marriage.

The Temple Family, Christmas 1977

The new house, 1964

House and Garden Harmony

Trudi has long understood that a strong visual tie between the sky, house and earth creates house-garden harmony. Just beyond a pumpkin patch, around a bend in the road, stood a lovely but lonely-looking house placed at the top of a knoll. When the house was built, Trudi kept track of its weekly progress, watching the people move in and eagerly awaiting the landscaping. Week after week—nothing.

Years went by and not a single tree or shrub was planted—only lawn, acres and acres of it. "Someone forgot to clothe the house," Trudi explains. She feels sad every time she drives past the house, standing naked and exposed to the elements.

If Trudi had been asked to dress the house, she'd have started with carefully placed trees and low-growing shrubs, then added plenty of perennials and annuals, window boxes, and vines growing up walls. She'd have connected the house to heaven and earth.

Today

Lily Flowering Tulips
(*Tulipa* 'Red Shine')

CHAPTER EIGHT

In Service

Trudi wanted to find time for her two passions—gardening and traveling. To satisfy her first love, she simply walked outside, put on gardening gloves and tackled a project in her untamed yard. Her delight in travel originated with childhood family trips to gardens in Germany and neighboring European countries. Since Bill was a United Airlines pilot, Trudi could travel inexpensively, flying stand-by for a nominal charge.

Bill and Trudi planned family trips to enrich their daughters' lives. However, their different travel styles made compromise a necessity. Bill liked his creature comforts—quality hotels, comfy beds and regular meals. Trudi, the adventurer, loved to "just wing it." She might sleep in her van and eat fruit, cheese, bread and boiled potatoes from her survival kit, traveling anywhere in the world without a care. They compromised. Once a year, Trudi planned a trip to a distant country, sometimes alone and sometimes with family or friends. These spontaneous trips, typically without prior reservations, usually turned out well as she made friends wherever she went. Trudianne commented, "For Mom, nobody's a stranger worldwide."

One example of this philosophy occurred recently. Traveling home in her van from a trip to the Southwest, Trudi stopped at a Missouri rest area for her last night's slumber. After a deep sleep, she woke up at six in the morning to a clatter. Looking through the window, she saw a tall garbage man emptying the overflowing trash cans. Trudi thought to herself, I just saved quite a bit of money on this trip by sleeping in my van and not paying for any hotel rooms, so why don't I give some to this man?

She left the van and said, "I just want to thank you for what you do for us," and handed him fifty dollars. Overwhelmed, he bent over, hugged her and said, "No one has ever thanked me before."

Trudi gets tears in her eyes as she tells this story, wishing she had done more.

❧

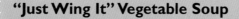
"Just Wing It" Vegetable Soup

6 cups cold water

1½ cups all-purpose flour

¼ cup chicken bouillon, vegetable bouillon granules or soup base

4–5 medium potatoes, any kind, peeled and diced into small cubes

Broccoli (Peel and cube stalks; save broccoli florets to add last.)

Cauliflower

2–3 tomatoes (Add whole into soup. After one minute, remove tomatoes and peel, then chop.)

Carrots

Green onions, celery, green pepper, beans, leeks and/or peas

Corn, fresh or canned

1 cup cooked ham, hot dogs or sausage, diced

½ cup onion sautéed (optional)

2–3 sprigs of fresh rosemary

1 t. oregano

1 T. Mrs. Dash® seasoning

Salt to taste

Pepper to taste

3–4 T. salsa, optional

1. In large soup pot, whisk together **cold** water and flour. Bring to boil, stirring frequently.

2. Add bouillon, potatoes, firm vegetables (stalks, carrots), meat and spices. Simmer about 10 minutes. Stir frequently. Check that potatoes are soft.

3. Add rest of vegetables and cook until soft.

4. Add broccoli florets and simmer 4 minutes.

5. Remove rosemary sprigs. Taste and correct spices. Add salt to taste. Add salsa if it needs a little more oomph.

Serves 8–10. Use your creativity and have fun with this recipe. It's a great way to use up leftovers. Make a vegetarian version by omitting the meat and using vegetable bouillon.

Trudianne and Trudi in Papua New Guinea

As soon as the girls were old enough, Trudi began taking one child with her on trips. An annual family tradition developed as Bill took one child and Trudi took the other on separate trips—in addition to family vacations. Those trips are cherished memories for Trudianne and Margo.

In January 1990, in the days of apartheid, Trudi and Margo traveled to South Africa. On a drive through the savannah near Johannesburg, they saw a young woman dressed in a long colorful skirt, white blouse and a straw hat. The woman stood alone, surrounded by a cardboard suitcase and several canvas bags.

Trudi slowed down and asked Margo, "Should we give her a ride?"

"Sure, she looks like a nice lady," Margo said.

They stopped and Trudi asked, "Do you need a ride?"

The woman smiled and said, "Oh, ma'am. That would be so nice. I'd be so grateful to you. I've been waiting for the bus to Soweto for hours."

Trudi knew Soweto, a huge area outside of Johannesburg, was reserved for the black population and was curious to see the town. On their way, the woman explained she was studying to be a nurse and hadn't been home in months. Her sweet personality and diligence impressed Trudi.

When the woman asked Trudi to drop her outside the village, Margo asked why they couldn't take her to her house. The nursing student explained that white people could run into danger in Soweto. Trudi still insisted on driving her all the way home.

When they reached the nursing student's small house, her husband came out to thank Trudi. Sensing the couple must be struggling to pay for her schooling, Trudi gave her several hundred dollars toward the next semester's tuition. The grateful couple warned Trudi to drive straight out of Soweto and not stop anywhere for anyone. Trudi didn't hesitate and left quickly. The nurse sent a letter thanking Trudi, assuring her she had used the money for school.

※

Each trip abroad, particularly when Trudi visited underdeveloped countries, renewed her deep desire to help less fortunate souls. But Trudi's determination to help others wasn't limited to people in foreign countries. One infamous family story took place on Christmas Eve. That morning, Trudi set the table for their annual party, expecting more than twenty guests. She looked out the kitchen window at the rapidly accumulating snow. All the food was prepared—huge platters of

Russian eggs with shrimp, ham, chicken drumsticks, stuffed mushrooms, deviled eggs and five different vegetables, all layered on top of German potato salad.

As the storm intensified, the phone began to ring. One after another, all the guests canceled until only the four family members were left to eat all the food. The girls, boggled by the mountains of food, weren't surprised when Bill asked, "Who is going to eat all this?"

Then she had a brainstorm. "I tell you what we'll do. We'll go to the highway and find stranded people and bring them here." Bill, a veteran of Trudi's great ideas, just rolled his eyes.

Trudianne and Margo chorused, "Mom, you can't do that."

Enthusiastic, Trudi responded, "Why not? Let's just go ahead and try it." Without much choice, everyone agreed as Trudi hurried into the kitchen to make even more food. What if they found fifty people?

At four o'clock, they left the house on their dinner crusade. Bill frowned as he drove, not saying a word. Trudianne and Margo kept repeating, "Who are we going to find?"

"I don't know. Let's start at the police station." The lone desk officer raised his eyebrows when Trudi told him her plan, then informed her the police station was deserted except for him. "Well," Trudi told him, "if you find anyone, just send them to us. Here's our address. We have plenty to eat."

Then they began cruising the highways looking for stranded motorists, but found none. Finally they stopped at the Hinsdale Oasis, an enclosed bridge over Interstate 294 housing a series of fast-food places. Trudi spotted four burly men in leather jackets smoking and laughing in the back of Burger King. As she started to walk toward them, Bill grabbed the hood of her jacket and whispered forcefully, "No!"

When Trudi looked at him, she saw a familiar look on his face and knew he wasn't going to budge. Just then she spotted a woman with long red hair wearing a short skirt, high black boots and a puffy jacket walk up to the counter. As Trudi started forward, Margo grabbed the hood of her mom's jacket, "Mom, get real!"

Every time Trudi found someone, either she was refused or one of her family objected. She couldn't make any headway with her family and was discouraged when they left with no one. A block from home, Bill slowed the car as he saw a lady in a pink parka trudging through the snow. Trudi perked up. "There's someone all by herself. Let's take her home, whoever she is." Bill stopped the car and she leaned out the window. "Excuse me. Are you by yourself tonight?"

The lady looked over at them. "Yes, I am."

Trudi recognized her. "Oh my gosh, it's Ruth. Come home with us for supper. We have lots of food." So their only guest was Ruth Law, a neighbor and famous cookbook author. The five of them feasted that night, but they still couldn't come close to consuming all the food.

The next Thanksgiving, an "Adopt A Sailor" program, was a more successful venture. Trudianne and Margo drove up to the Great Lakes Naval Station north of Chicago, picked out two sailors and brought them home on Thanksgiving Day. Bringing home cute sailors was certainly more to their liking than Trudi's Christmas crusade had been.

❧

Always aware of the needy, Trudi acted despite the circumstances. One Sunday afternoon in February, Trudi was eating at a Taco Bell in Chicago with two German friends. The only other person in the restaurant, a grey-haired man in worn jeans and thin cotton jacket, sat alone, cradling a cup of coffee. With her friends' backs to him, they couldn't see him staring at Trudi so fiercely that she became intimidated. As she wondered what she should do, he kept staring.

Trudi felt her heart pounding as beads of sweat trickled down her back. Were they going to be mugged? Above all, she wanted to protect her visitors; she had to do something.

Then it occurred to Trudi that maybe he was just hungry. In the middle of eating a beef burrito, she abruptly got up from the table and walked over to him. "Are you hungry?" she asked.

"Yes." He hung his head.

Were they going to be mugged?

"Go and help yourself to whatever you want. I'll be happy to take care of it." His astonishment quickly changed to a smile when he saw Trudi meant what she said. The man got up, ordered and returned to his seat with one taco. She walked over to him again. "Well, I just don't think that's enough. Go back and load up your tray." This time he did.

Trudi knew Bill thought she was crazy when she did this kind of thing. He worried even more when she was alone, yet she couldn't resist stopping the day she saw a car pulled over on the side of the road. "What's the matter?" Trudi asked a young man with shaggy black hair.

"I ran out of gas."

"That's no problem. I can go get gas."

"That's not the only problem I have. I don't have any money," he said softly, looking down at his tattered sneakers.

"That's no problem either." Trudi drove him to the nearest gas station where she bought a can of gas and returned to his car without incident.

Fearless, Trudi never thought of her own safety.

Not everyone in trouble needed money. During a blizzard, Trudi drove along a divided four-lane highway near home and almost hit a car stopped on the shoulder. The storm's poor visibility had shrouded it from view. Pulling off the road, she got out and asked the elderly couple, "What's the problem?"

"Our car stopped. Nothing works."

"I can help you. I'll back up behind you, put on my flashers and wait with you until the tow truck comes." They sat for an hour, waiting. Trudi listened to the radio, walked to the stranded car several times to check on the couple and drove away when the tow truck came.

She never told the couple her name. Bill heard the story twice, once from Trudi and again at his Rotary meeting the next week, when a fellow Rotarian praised the kind stranger. Bill proudly admitted, "That was my wife."

❦

Trudi's trip abroad in 1972 didn't involve an act of kindness, but set the stage for years of service to others. She and her friend, Patsy Cushing, went to the South China Sea. Without hotel reservations, they flew to Hong Kong and immediately began looking for lodging. Trudi was thrilled to find a hotel on Twist Street with rooms for $1.50 a night. She said to Patsy, "Boy, this is great! The price is right."

The next morning Trudi awoke to the sounds of Patsy packing. "What's the matter?" she asked.

"Look at your bedside table." Trudi had put little packages of crackers and cheese—saved from the flight—on the table. Mice had eaten them and left evidence of their theft—droppings everywhere. "I'm moving up one dollar," Patsy announced, and they found a room for $2.50 a night.

Like most other Hong Kong tourists, Trudi and Patsy couldn't wait to go shopping. In one small gift shop, the Chinese lady behind the counter, Mrs. Yip, was extraordinarily friendly. They began chatting with her and ended up spending the entire morning in her shop. Mrs. Yip invited Trudi and Patsy to lunch at a restaurant with a long line of people waiting for tables. As soon as she snapped her fingers, they were seated. Impressed to see Mrs. Yip treated like royalty, Trudi knew she must be someone special. "What does your husband do, Mrs. Yip?" she inquired.

"You'll never guess."

Trudi loved guessing games and tried her hardest to figure out Mr. Yip's occupation. When she finally gave up, Mrs. Yip enlightened her. "He is a Presbyterian minister. The store you were in is one of seven stores belonging to a benevolent corporation. All the money we make goes for church and mission work."

Captivated by their life of service, Trudi and Patsy eagerly accepted her dinner invitation. At dinner, Pastor Yip explained that he was an innovator, the force behind getting the work week reduced from seven days to six for Chinese workers in Hong Kong. Because entire families lived in one room and slept in shifts, they couldn't all stay home on their new day off. Pastor Yip started a day-off program with cultural activities for the families.

The next day the Yips drove Patsy and Trudi to a youth center that had been built by the benevolent corporation. Waiting for a red light to change, Trudi suddenly felt a powerful surge of spiritual energy. She sensed approval—almost as though she were being told, "You are on the right track. Just listen and be alert." Completely bewildered, Trudi didn't know what to think, but from that moment on, she felt a guiding presence.

> ... she felt a guiding presence.

After Patsy and Trudi went on to Thailand, Trudi radically changed her plans. Instead of returning home with Patsy, Trudi went back to Hong Kong and spent three more days with the Yips. They asked her to accompany them on a visit to a refugee camp on an island in the South China Sea. The refugees, having escaped from Red China, lived there while the pastor and his wife tried to find jobs and housing for them in Hong Kong.

Trudi sat on bags of chicken feed as they sailed for three hours on a Chinese junk before boarding a much smaller sampan to reach the island. Stepping off the sampan, she saw many tiny huts, with squawking chickens and oinking pigs running everywhere. The cook, who had come with them, began dinner preparations by grabbing a few chickens and whacking off their heads. After a short wait, the host presented the guests with a mug containing clear broth with a raw egg at the bottom. Trudi thought, Oh, brother! She knew drinking the delicacy was a polite necessity and quickly gulped it down. Impressed that she had finished it so quickly, they presented Trudi with a second mug. Unable to stomach another round, Trudi cradled the mug in her hands until she could dump it near a roaming pig.

After a remarkable dinner, Trudi learned the Yips had begun constructing little houses on Kowloon for the families of fishermen. They explained that many poverty-stricken Chinese, unable to afford to settle on land, lived on their sampans, small boats propelled by sail or an oar from the stern. With woven mats forming a small cabin, entire extended families jammed all their worldly goods onto these rickety vessels. They subsisted in floating villages of sampans and junks, larger ocean-going fishing vessels. The adults fished to support the family. Each year, when the violent typhoons struck, the force of wind and water destroyed many sampans, often killing entire families.

For $700, the Yips could build a one-room dwelling for a family. Then the little children and elderly grandparents could stay home, while the younger generations braved the seas.

This mission project inspired Trudi; her future path seemed clear.

Back home, Trudi wanted to raise money for the Yips' mission. She wondered what she could do. With two small children, she didn't want a full-time job. One evening, while soaking in her bathtub, her favorite thinking place, she realized the solution grew in her garden. After nine years, she had amassed a large, unusual plant collection. She could sell some of her plants, but how?

A few days later, Trudi overheard a man at the local garden center talking loudly to a salesperson and becoming more and more irritated. Each plant he asked for was unavailable. Finally, he began swearing in German. Trudi, understanding every word he said, was amused. Realizing how frustrated the man was, she walked over to him and said, "Sir, every plant you asked for is in my garden. I would love to share them with you."

He explained he was a landscape contractor trying to construct a large rock garden. After he followed her home, they loaded up his car with plants. Embarrassed she had heard him swear, he apologized profusely. When ready to leave, he asked, "How much do I owe you?"

"Nothing. Just take them, one countryman to another." Trudi didn't feel right charging a fellow German. After he left, she fretted that she had missed her chance. She could have made some money to give to the mission.

A few days later, a check for twenty-five dollars arrived from the woman who had commissioned the garden. Elated, Trudi sent her first check to Hong Kong.

South Water Street Market

At that moment, Trudi's small home industry was born. She used flowers from her garden to make floral arrangements for parties and weddings, and word spread that the profit would go to mission work. Besides providing the flowers for her church, soon Trudi was arranging flowers for three other churches each Saturday. For Mother's Day 1972, she advertised in her church bulletin that she would make corsages. Everyone loved Trudi's creations and told their friends about this unique opportunity. The following Mother's Day, Trudi filled orders for 115 corsages and thought her fingers might fall off.

After the first frost killed her flowers, Trudi tried to make deals with the local florists for flowers at reasonable prices, offering to give them cut flowers from her garden the next summer if they would supply her in the winter. They turned down her deal.

Trudi knew there must be a place she could buy inexpensive flowers. When a florist told her about the wholesale market on Randolph Street, she began driving into Chicago early in the morning, long before rush hour. Timid at first about finding her way around Chicago before dawn, Trudi slowly became comfortable.

By January 1973, Trudi had gained enough confidence to explore the other Chicago markets. A few blocks from the flower market, she discovered the noisy, bustling produce stalls. Store fronts opened onto truckers' loading docks as beeping forklifts moved giant bags of potatoes, cartons of leaf lettuce and boxes of oranges onto the waiting trucks. Once inside, she barely noticed the muddy sawdust floors as she marveled at case after case of perfect fruits and vegetables.

This is fantastic, she thought, and bought thirteen cases of produce, including shiny red apples, fragrant oranges, plump green pears, forty pounds of bananas, perfect leaf lettuce, broccoli, cauliflower, potatoes and grapes. Jubilant, Trudi never considered she had bought enough produce for forty instead of four.

When Bill came home that afternoon, he took one look at the mountain of food on their long kitchen table and raised his eyebrows. "What is this?"

"The most wonderful fresh fruits and vegetables—and very inexpensive!"

Sensible Bill said, "We can't possibly eat all of this. You'd better call your friends and share it." Trudi called five friends who each took a portion. With too much remaining, she called her neighbors at the Institute in Basic Life Principles, and they took half of her remaining portion. She sold it to them at her cost.

A few days later, her friends called back. "That was a terrific deal," they all agreed. "Could you do it again?"

"Sure, I go downtown to get flowers every Friday anyway, so I could get the produce then. Give me your orders by Thursday."

"That would be perfect."

Trudi told her friends that her final portion of the produce had been so large she had shared it with the Institute. They each confessed they, too, had shared theirs.

❧

Initially Trudi's plan was ideal, because each case of produce easily divided into twelve parts. To keep her ordering simple at the market, she never took special orders, with the exception of whole cases. Everyone got the same thing—a mixed box of top-quality fruits and vegetables. Good news travels fast. Others found out about the co-op and were added to a waiting list until another group of twelve was formed. Every Friday Trudi lugged the cases home—never charging anything extra, not even for gas.

Pat Ryan, who later became one of Trudi's first sales representatives, remembers meeting her on a Friday afternoon. While visiting one of Trudi's customers, Pat drove over to Trudi's house to pick up her friend's order, stacked in the driveway. She noticed a cigar box used to collect payments and a black-and-white composition notebook to record next week's order.

One of the co-op's customers, Gene Haak, had met the Yips during their fundraising trip to America when they visited Trudi and Bill. He said, "Trudi, I don't understand you. You're running around trying to make money for Pastor Yip while you've got a business right here. Charge a little something for this service so you can make some money for your missions."

What a great idea, Trudi thought. Since tithing to a church is 10 percent, she decided to add that much to her wholesale bills. When she proposed this new arrangement to her customers, they all agreed.

Trudi's business grew quickly, all by word of mouth, and she happily served more area customers. Many of them were young families with small children, and all loved the quality and convenience of Trudi's food.

When the amount of flowers and produce outgrew her station wagon, Trudi borrowed a van on Fridays. Getting bolder by the week, she explored all the Chicago wholesale markets and discovered

The new refrigerator

meats, cheeses, seafood, bread and even Christmas ribbon—all the things she could use for her family. Sometimes Trudi would experiment. She purchased a new item, such as a five-pound brick of sliced American cheese, to see if anyone would buy it. If they didn't, great, she had it for her family. Without fail, each time Trudi purchased something new, one of her customers bought it. Delighted, she added more and more items.

When summer came, Trudi had a new worry—perishables. She shared this problem with one of her customers; a few days later, Trudi's phone rang. "I heard you need a refrigerator. I have a brand-new Sears fridge that no one seems to be able to fix. If your husband is handy, maybe he can figure out what's wrong and you can have it." Trudi knew Bill's best friend, Clay Doty, could fix anything. After the broken refrigerator arrived, Clay and Bill discovered a twelve-dollar part needed replacing. Trudi had a new refrigerator.

⁂

By 1975, Trudi had expanded her business to eighty-four families, the maximum she could handle. She made anywhere from $125 to $150 a week in profit, all designated for mission work. Pastor Yip received a substantial grant from the World Council of Churches that year, so Trudi found other projects that needed help, including Lake Bluff Children's Home, the Redbird Mission in Kentucky, New Tribes Mission in Borneo and Hinsdale Community Service in her hometown.

Even more than sending a check to a charity, Trudi loved meeting those who needed help. That summer, while trying to wait patiently in a long airport line to check her luggage, she peered around the snaking line to see what the problem was. Two adults with five children and multiple suitcases were holding up the line. Trudi noticed the mother and daughters wearing long-sleeved blouses and ankle-length skirts, with their long hair neatly tied back, and surmised they were missionaries. Leaving her place in line, she walked up and asked them. "What's going on?"

"We're on our way to Africa to be missionaries in the bush," the man explained. "It's really isolated and there aren't any schools, so we teach our children ourselves. The schoolbooks have made our luggage too heavy and we owe $129 for the excess weight. We don't have the extra money to pay the fee." With great satisfaction, Trudi pulled out her new business checkbook and paid for the baggage.

The grateful missionaries sent her a special letter from Africa expressing their thanks.

Antique railroad luggage cart
Licorice Plant *(Helichrysum petiolatum)*
Lady Fern *(Asplenium felix-femina)*
Hybrid Fuchsia
Variegated Spider Plant *(Chlorophytum comosum* 'Vittatum'*)*
Ivy Geranium *(Pelargonium peltatum)*

A planter box made from recycled wood
is a summer home for house plants.

Tree stump
Variegated Shell Ginger *(Alpinia zerumbet*
'Variegata'*)*

GARDEN TIP

Creative Containers

Containers must be large for the healthiest plants and most creative garden design. Unfortunately, most commercially available planters are too small. They dry out so quickly during a hot summer that keeping the soil moist and the plants healthy becomes a real challenge; the plants can die without daily watering.

Making a container can be as easy as nailing a few boards together to make a box. Attach four legs, place the container between plants in your garden and fill it with enriched soil. Trudi uses horse manure, aged two to three years. (Fresh manure will kill plants.) An alternative is a mixture of packaged mushroom compost, aged cow manure, sand and garden soil.

Play with textures in combining your favorite upright and cascading plants in containers. Try adding house plant in your design. Consider moisture, soil and light requirements in grouping plants.

Old iron lawn chair
Wormwood *(Artemesia* 'Powis Castle'*)*
Angel-Wing Begonia *(Begonia* 'Lucerna'*)*
Coleus 'Peridot' *(Solenostemon scutellarioides* 'Peridot'*)*
Lantana *(Lantana camara* 'Tangerine'*)*
Coleus 'Swinging Linda' *(Solenostemon scutellarioides* 'Swinging Linda'*)*

Old washtub at the farm
Chrysanthemum
Swiss Chard *(Beta vulgaris* var. *cicla)*
Ornamental Cabbage *(Brassica oleracea)*
Kale *(Brassica oleracea* var. *acephala)*

115

Peony 'America' *(Paeonia 'America')*

PART THREE

MARKET DAY

Hosta *(H.* 'Gold Standard'*)*
Christmas Fern *(Polystichum acrostichoides)*
Weeping Norway Spruce *(Picea abies* 'Pendula'*)*

Growth

Masterwort *(Astrantia major* 'Rosea'*)*

Sometimes a momentous change tiptoes in so quietly the critical decision seems almost mundane. Picture Trudianne, a fifth-grader, sitting down at the kitchen table for an after-school snack in April 1975. "Mom, our class is having a bake sale tomorrow to raise money for the learning center. Can you bake a cake today?"

Instead of her usual positive response, Trudi was as surprised as Trudianne when she answered, "No."

Trudianne was stunned. "You won't bake a cake?"

"You know I bake cakes from scratch. I'm not going to spend five dollars on ingredients when they sell pieces for twenty-five cents!"

Trudianne began to cry, upset her mother didn't even give her the option of an appeal. Hastily Trudi thought of an alternative. "I'll tell you what I'll do. I'll give you ten dollars for your fundraiser."

That made Trudianne even unhappier. She pleaded, "I'll be the only one without a cake."

Margo, only six, came to her sister's aid. "I can help, Mama."

Trudi was adamant and actually raised her voice to silence them. Now they were both sobbing—unusual for a family not used to arguing. The girls couldn't wait for their father to come home to tell him the story.

As soon as Bill walked in the door, the two red-eyed girls ran to him. He looked at Trudi in disbelief. "What is going on here?" he asked.

She rattled off, "They want me to bake a cake, and I don't want to bake a cake that will sell for half its cost, and Trudianne won't take the ten dollars and I'm just not going to bake a cake!"

Once Bill had the whole story, he agreed with the girls. "Trudi, you cannot send Trudianne with ten dollars when everyone else is bringing a cake."

Trudi wouldn't budge. "I'm not going to bake a cake."

Trudianne and her mom

Obsttorte (fruit torte)

6 large eggs, separated
1 cup sugar
1 T. vanilla extract
1²/₃ cups all-purpose flour
³/₄ cup grape or currant jelly
Variety of fruit: canned pineapple slices, peaches or mandarin oranges, well-drained; fresh kiwi slices, berries or pitted cherries
4 t. arrowroot
¹/₄ cup sugar
2 cups of juice from canned fruit
¹/₃ cup finely ground almonds, walnuts or pecans

1. Preheat the oven to 375°. Line bottom of 10-inch springform pan with foil. Place sides on pan and close clasp. Carefully grease sides and foiled bottom of pan with butter or margarine.

2. In large, deep mixing bowl, beat egg whites to stiff peaks. With mixer on low speed, slowly add sugar. Beat at high speed.

3. Beat egg yolks with a whisk. Slowly add to egg whites.

4. Sift flour into bowl. Gently fold flour into batter with a rubber spatula. Work quickly. Do not beat. (Air is the only rising agent in this recipe; this step is key.)

5. Pour batter into prepared pan. Place in preheated oven. Bake for 50–60 minutes or until top is golden brown. Do not open oven while cake is baking, or it could fall.

6. Remove cake from oven, place on rack and cool for ten minutes. Loosen edges of cake with knife before removing sides of pan. Flip cake over onto cake rack, remove bottom of pan and peel off foil.

7. When cake is totally cool, cut it in half horizontally. Place one half on large serving platter, cut side up. To save the other half for another time, wrap it tightly and freeze.

8. Spread jelly on top of the cake in a thin layer. Place the fruit on top of the jelly in a pleasing design.

9. Glaze. Mix arrowroot and sugar in a small bowl. Set aside. Place 2 cups of fruit juice in pot. Bring to a boil. Stir in sugar mixture. Return to a boil and cook until thick and clear, stirring continuously.

10. Spoon glaze over fruit until it runs down the sides of the cake. Use knife to spread glaze from plate up onto sides of cake. Sprinkle nuts around outside 1" of cake top and onto sides.

"All right," said Bill. "You cannot send ten dollars and you won't bake a cake. Well then, think of something better."

No peace in the house that night. There had to be a way, Trudi thought, lying awake in bed. By morning she had figured it out. "Hey, Trudianne, I have an idea. You know the co-op that I run out of the garage?"

"Yes."

"I will give you the profits from a co-op sale. We'll invite all the parents and teachers to a big sale at the school."

Trudianne suspiciously looked up at her mother. "How much money will we make?"

"I'm sure we'll make about two hundred dollars."

That perked her up. Trudianne went to her principal, Dr. Tom Hughes, that same day and explained why her mother wouldn't bake a cake. After calling Trudi and hearing her explanation, Dr. Hughes's confusion turned to enthusiasm. "Let's go for it. Sounds wonderful," he agreed.

Margo excitedly told Leslie Goddard, her best friend, about the food sale. Leslie's mother, Carol, called Trudi and offered to help. After Trudi two-finger-typed a little order sheet with about twelve of her best-selling items, the school took orders from the parents and staff. Trudi asked all her Friday customers to pick up their orders at the school that week. She then borrowed a truck to deliver the food. Volunteers helped sort the food, preparing the orders for pickup. The sale raised $328.10 for the Walker School, much to everyone's delight.

It never occurred to Trudi she'd have another school sale until two weeks later when Dr. Hughes phoned. "Trudi, I've gotten call after call from the parents who bought food at your sale. They want to do it again." Trudi discussed it with Bill, who served on the school board. With intimate knowledge of the school district's need for money, Bill encouraged the sale, volunteering to take care of the girls. Soon after that, the principals from Monroe School in Hinsdale and Prospect School in Clarendon Hills called to ask if they, too, could have sales. Trudi had taken her business to a new level.

She named her business "True These Benefit Marketing," because Trudi's Benefit Marketing was already taken. The name was such a tongue twister Trudi shortened it to Benefit Marketing, a better choice as it reflected her goal of running a market benefiting everyone.

An Appeal

Bill and Trudi presented a united front on the important rules—with a special twist intended to teach the girls to think logically. They gave their daughters one appeal if Bill or Trudi said no to something desired. Trudianne or Margo then had time to go to her room and think before she came back to them with her reasoned argument. Trudi and Bill listened to the appeal; sometimes they changed their minds and sometimes they didn't.

The answer to the appeal was final.

The alley

Although Trudi had stretched her comfort zone repeatedly throughout her life, she was about to take her courage to a new level. Leaving home at 1:30 a.m., she drove her van down to Chicago's Randolph Street Market. Enduring many miserable, icy Chicago winter nights, Trudi slogged through grey slush wearing big fat moon boots to keep her feet warm. She turned her jacket's collar up against the wind and tucked her long hair into a knit cap—a unisex look. But was this enough to keep her safe?

Trudi's family would have been horrified if they had known about her route to the wholesale markets. In this early phase of her business, she carried cash through some of the most notorious Chicago neighborhoods. After parking on a dim street in the shadows of a low-income public housing project, she had to walk up treacherous, slippery steps and along a deserted loading dock—the worst part of her journey. Alone in the darkness, Trudi walked briskly, trying to ignore the menacing silence.

She entered a giant, gloomy warehouse filled with mountains of produce cartons. Keenly aware of her surroundings, she noticed every sound until she exited the warehouse. Closer to the market, Trudi heard the comforting chaos of trucks, sirens, shouted orders and honking horns. After descending steps to an odorous, dark alley filled with hulking delivery trucks and littered with debris, she finally climbed uneven steps to her destination.

After months of that weekly nightmare, Trudi made friends with Jimmy, a night watchman at one of the produce loading docks. Aware of her vulnerability, he made sure to help her cross the alley and reach the haven of the colorful produce market.

❧

Trudi always selected the freshest products—only the finest quality would do for her customers. One night she carefully picked out one lot of two hundred flats of strawberries, a special order for a school's strawberry festival. When the strawberries were delivered to her truck, she realized they were not the ones she had chosen and called the vendor. "You've got to come get these strawberries. I want the lot I picked out."

"Yeah, be right there," the man said in a bored voice.

Constantly under a deadline, Trudi had to be home in time to get the girls off to school and then deliver to the schools. After several more calls, she gave him an ultimatum, "I give you half an hour to change these strawberries. If you don't come, I'm going to walk away and I will no longer be responsible for them." She waited the thirty minutes and then left to buy strawberries elsewhere. After the berries disappeared, the vendor tried to make Trudi pay for them; she refused.

At this point, Trudi was selling a mixed box of produce of her own choosing for nine dollars. Her supermarket price comparison showed the produce was worth approximately fifteen dollars. A typical medley contained apples, pears, grapes, oranges, grapefruit, lemons, bananas, spinach, cauliflower, zucchini, carrots, broccoli, lettuce and green onions. One box of produce contributed eighty cents to her fundraising efforts—10 percent over cost.

Sorting produce

One man actually told Trudi to her face that her little business was "a really dumb idea." He didn't understand that she had not gone into business to make money for herself; her goal was to donate money to those not as privileged as she was. However small her first donations, they added up. In a typical week in May 1975, Trudi donated $65.65 to Hinsdale Community Service.

That first summer Pat Ryan—who had kept in touch with Trudi—eagerly anticipated a sale to benefit the school in her hometown, Crystal Lake. For Trudi's first distant sale, she drove ahead of a large produce truck northwest from Chicago on I-90. Misreading a sign, she turned south toward Geneva instead of north toward Lake Geneva. After frantically calling Pat, she finally showed up in Crystal Lake an hour late, just in time to greet the customers arriving to pick up their orders. That day, instead of the typical orderly pickup, everyone pitched in to help sort the food into boxes.

✁

Trudi with the guys at the market

Men dominated the wholesale markets in the 1970s. Most were devout Catholics. They treated the only other woman, a nun, with great deference. In their eyes, she could do no wrong. Trudi was different. In the beginning, when she needed ten pounds of mushrooms, they could afford to ignore her. Before long, as her orders grew to two hundred pounds of mushrooms, they paid more attention.

The offensive language Trudi heard in her early days at the Chicago market upset her, and she tried to ignore it. But by the time she was buying thousands of dollars worth of goods instead of hundreds, she knew she had more clout. Gradually Trudi let it be known that she didn't appreciate the swearing. Though the men weren't sure what to make of her, she soon noticed a difference. They yelled, "Trudi's here!" when they saw her and cleaned up their language.

Bill didn't ask about the conditions at the markets, and Trudi never told him. He wanted her to be happy and knew she loved her business. She always had his full support, even though he never played an active part in Trudi's venture.

Time-Saving Tips

Set the table

Set the table for dinner in the morning, even before you have any idea of what the meal will be. Add some flowers and a few candles. The impact is phenomenal. When your family walks in and sees a nicely set dining room table, everyone smiles.

Use commercial time

When you're watching television, use a commercial break as a signal for action: write a few checks, fold the laundry or water some plants. Collect the garbage during one break and take it out during the next. Do some push-ups or stretches. If you're watching a long movie, it's amazing how much you can do.

Five-minute power

Five minutes is a long time. Many people just doodle time away instead of spotting something that needs doing and taking five minutes to make a start. Using a hoe, Trudi can weed a small garden bed in just five minutes. The trick is grabbing that time and focusing on a task.

Often Trudi thought, I can't believe what I'm doing. She was doing everything at that point: driving into Chicago, picking out food, loading her truck, driving home, taking care of her family, then delivering food to the sales. The schools' volunteers divided the produce and set up for the sales with Trudi's supervision.

Trudianne and Margo didn't realize how hard their mother was working, because she was always there for them during the day. Even though she was getting only two to three hours of sleep on the nights she drove into Chicago, Trudi was home to get them breakfast and put them on the bus before starting her deliveries.

When Trudi came home in the afternoon, the first thing she did was set the table to create a positive atmosphere. When Bill, Trudianne and Margo arrived, they saw the table all set for dinner and thought Trudi had everything under control. On particularly busy days, she could quickly make soup or serve a leftover. Her girls fondly remember their mother's creative "munchie plates." When Bill was away on overnight trips, Trudi scavenged in the refrigerator for finger foods such as bite-sized hamburger patties, rolled-up cold cuts, vegetable sticks, rye bread with mayonnaise and radishes, and bowls of peas in butter sauce. She spread a bed sheet on the living room floor in front of the television and handed the girls chopsticks, which they actually learned to use. This television banquet kept them occupied the rest of the evening.

❧

From the start in 1972, Bill had paid all the expenses of Trudi's growing business. In 1976, he finally told Trudi, "Your business is getting too expensive for me. Don't give away all the profits. Keep some of the money and pay your own expenses."

Not wanting to shortchange the missions, Trudi needed a plan to increase her income. She decided to ask for a 3 percent cash rebate and called a meeting at the market to tell the vendors about her mission work and her need to cover expenses. All agreed, except the meat vendor. "My boss never gives rebates," he said. Trudi thought, OK, I'll get my rebate from everyone else and still be able to pay my expenses.

When the owner of the meat company heard Trudi gave all her profits to missions, he contacted her. "Trudi, I heard that my people won't give you your 3 percent rebate. That's right, but I've got a better idea to help you out." He told her he was dying of cancer and wanted to straighten out things in his life. True to his word, he hired Trudi as a sales representative and gave her a 4 percent commission; she was her only customer. The kind owner died soon after their meeting.

Once Trudi had enough money to cover her expenses, she hired a secretary, the efficient Shirley Masuka. Trudi explains, "She wasn't just my secretary; she was my everything. When Bill was working and I was late getting home in the morning, she braided the girls' hair, made them lunch, sent them off to school or welcomed them home. She sat in our dining room and did my paperwork for a year."

Eventually Bill began to complain, "I'm tired of your secretary in our dining room. I want to be able to come downstairs in the morning in my pajamas." Because the business had grown so rapidly, Trudi could afford to build a small office in half of the garage, where Shirley worked diligently for several years.

Soon Trudi admitted she couldn't do it all and hired more sales representatives. While she still ran the smaller sales, the reps managed the larger ones. With the help of volunteers, they set up for the sales, sorted the food and divided it into each customer's purchase, organizing about seventy-five sales a month during the school year.

Every June, when schools went on summer vacation, Trudi invited all the sales reps to a year-end luncheon at her house to reinforce their close ties. Pat Ryan, one of Trudi's most trusted and positive sales reps, became a dear friend.

Trudi drove into Chicago almost every night to buy products for increasing numbers of fundraising events benefiting schools, churches and other nonprofit organizations. She also ran sales for families in need, including a local family whose house burned down and a new Cambodian refugee family arriving in town without any furniture or winter clothing.

Despite the exhausting hard work, something always happened to brighten Trudi's spirits and reenergize her. One day Bill provided that spark. Trudi did all her calculations by hand. When calculators came on the market, she wanted one badly, but they were too expensive, $265. After mentioning her wish to Bill, he said, "Just set some money aside and buy one."

Trudi refused, "I wouldn't dream of spending that kind of money on a convenience."

One day, soon after their discussion, Bill walked into the kitchen, beaming. With his hands hidden behind his back, he said, "I won a door prize at the Rotary meeting."

"That's nice. What did you get?"

He proudly presented Trudi with a brand-new, handheld calculator. Thrilled, she gave him a big hug.

After years of daily use, Trudi actually wore the numbers off that invaluable calculator.

Inspiring Loyalty

Trudi wanted to avoid a boss-employee barrier as much as possible, so she treated all her employees as equals. She demonstrated a positive, "can do" approach for her employees and tried never to ask them to work any harder than she did herself.

She followed the military adage: praise in public; punish in private.

She dressed for her surroundings in neat, everyday clothing, remembering her father's caution, "Be more than you show."

The Trial Garden

Trudi loves her hidden garden, a combination vegetable and trial garden. It has a ceiling. Fifteen years ago, during one particularly frustrating summer, birds and other small animals devoured nearly all of her berries and vegetables. At wit's end, Trudi told Bill she wanted to cage in the whole vegetable garden, using chain link to create the top and sides of the cage. She planned to sink plastic sheeting into the ground around the perimeter so the "crafty critters" couldn't dig into the garden. Bill commented, "You'll have to live two hundred years to make that a worthwhile project." Trudi did it anyway and was delighted with the result. The next year Bill had to admit the raspberries had never tasted so good.

A huge "Trudi pit" is always in progress in the trial garden. After it's filled to overflowing, Trudi covers it with wood chips and turns it into a walkway. Two to three years later, she adds soil and it becomes a raised bed. Primroses thrive at the edge of these beds and vegetables flourish on top.

Trudi lines some of the walkways with one-gallon plastic pots filled with soil and sunk into the ground. When she finds a special volunteer seedling or a leftover perennial division she wants to save, she plants it in a waiting container. When mature, these plants can be used as gifts, traded with another gardener or used to fill gaps in a planter, window box or garden bed at blooming time. Since these plants have been grown in containers outdoors, they are more portable and suffer less transplant shock.

127

Coleus sp. *(Solenostemon scutellarioides)*
Boston Fern *(Nephrolepis exalta* 'Bostoniensis'*)*

Primrose *(Primula vulgaris)*

The Monster

When Trudi's van became too small, she bought a step-van, the size of a bread truck.

She was driving it when the steak snafu occurred. Several weeks before Christmas, a Rotary Club ordered thirty boxes of steaks. With the meat in her step-van, Trudi called for delivery instructions. The woman sounded perplexed. "That's nice, except you have the wrong week. Our order was for next week."

"No problem. I'll bring them next week." Trudi answered pleasantly, while thinking, Oh, brother.

Her frustration didn't dampen her determination that those steaks wouldn't go to waste. Late that afternoon, Trudi asked Bill and the girls to help her ferry them from the truck to their freezer in the basement. After a few trips, Trudi still had a huge stack of boxes to unload when a school called. They needed her right away. She hopped into the truck and took off. Careening around the first turn onto Ogden Avenue, she suddenly remembered the open roll-up door. She swung into a parking lot, jumped out of the cab and ran around to look into the truck. Not one box was left.

Frantic, Trudi peeled back out onto Ogden Avenue. Her headlights hit the steak boxes, strewn across four lanes of rush-hour traffic. Quickly swinging the truck across traffic and blocking all four lanes, she started gathering up steaks, even those already smashed by people driving over them.

A tow truck driver pulled up to her, red lights flashing. That driver, then others, got out of their cars to help her pick up the steaks and toss them into her truck. Embarrassed, Trudi thanked everyone and drove home.

At home, Trudi told Bill the tale and said, "We're going to eat an awful lot of steak."

He raised his eyebrows, "We can't possibly eat them all!"

After many phone calls and laughter, their friends came over and bought all the steaks that weren't tire-tenderized. Trudi refused to waste even those. She washed them off, froze them and eventually served them to her family, tire tracks and all.

Loading a borrowed van

The girls play in the truck.

When she outgrew the step-van, Trudi borrowed larger trucks, loading and unloading them all by herself. One night at South Water Market, she found something to save her back, a discarded section of a conveyor belt leaning against the wall. The owner sold it to Trudi for fifteen dollars—her Mother's Day present to herself.

Trudianne and Margo loved the new plaything. Trudi set it up on the truck; the girls found an empty box, jumped in and raced down the incline, just like her food boxes.

By this time Trudi was driving to three markets—Randolph Street, Fulton Street, and South Water Street—and making thirteen stops in all each night. She picked up bread at one place, fish at another, then cheese, sausage and produce—each at a different stop. Trudi loved the bakery that sold French bread. Even though she made little profit on it, Trudi wanted her customers to have the best French bread in Chicago. The bakery just happened to be the last stop before she headed home, and she often treated herself to a snack, a chunk of liver sausage squeezed onto bread still warm from the bakery's oven.

One morning at six a.m., Trudi was on her way home from the Randolph Street Market when she suddenly heard people screaming, "Fire, fire, fire!"

A car pulled up next to her. "Stop! You're on fire!" the driver yelled.

Trudi jammed on the brakes and jumped out to find a fire under the truck. People came running out of their houses with fire extinguishers as someone called the fire department. By the time help arrived, the fire was extinguished but the firemen told her the truck couldn't be driven.

Leaning over the steering wheel, Trudi wilted as she muttered, "Great. The truck is loaded with food and I have deadlines to meet. Now what?"

Just at that moment, an angel appeared in the form of a heavy-set African-American man. He walked across the street and said, "I think that was just an oil fire because the truck is dirty. You can still drive. I'll help you out. Where do you need to go?" When she told him, he said, "I'll follow you just in case the fire starts again."

After following her almost all the way home, he waved as he drove off. Trudi comments, "What a nice man and I never even knew his name."

One night in Chicago, Trudi had another terrible scare. At 3 a.m., she drove her truck on West Madison, past boarded-up, graffiti-covered buildings, and stopped at a red light. A group of men surrounded the truck. One jumped on the running board right next to her. Trudi knew she was in trouble and thought, Thank heavens the truck's locked. She leaned on the horn, put the truck in gear, drove through the men and sped through the intersection, ignoring the red light.

For days, Trudi searched the newspaper to see if someone had been killed. She never found anything—a huge relief. After that, she avoided West Madison Street.

❧

Trudi dreaded dealing with Gus, the meat company's irritable manager. After she became friendly with the drivers who delivered to restaurants, one took her aside and said, "I've noticed Gus is charging you five cents more per pound for the hamburger than he's charging me. Don't tell him I told you."

Furious, Trudi marched up to his desk and confronted him. He denied it and without proof, she could do nothing. She spied another driver's bill of sale lying on a counter. Grabbing the paper, she stomped over to Gus and slapped the receipt down on the counter. "Here is the proof that you're charging me more than all the others."

Livid she had caught him, Gus picked up the paper and turned on Trudi. He yelled back, two inches from her face, "You suburban whore! You get the hell out of here and don't ever come back!"

Trudi got out without her meat order and sat in her truck sobbing, the first time she had ever wept over her business. After collecting herself, she decided to look for another meat-packing company that same night. At a new meat market, she found the manager so friendly she burst into tears again, right in front of the stranger. He didn't know what to do with her or why she was crying. Embarrassed, Trudi turned on her heel and left.

She paged through the telephone books the next day for yet another new meat-packing company that met her standards. The first company sold her meat in plastic bags with inches of fresh blood pooled in the bottom. Disappointed, Trudi thought, This meat hasn't been aged properly. I can't possibly take it. Standing at the counter, Trudi gathered her courage and told the manager she simply couldn't accept this large order he had cut especially for her. Again she had to tell her customers there was no meat.

Finally, Trudi was forced to admit to herself that Gus's company sold the best meat. Deciding her customers deserved the finest quality, even at the expense of her pride, she returned to him with an apology. "Gus, you know last month, when I confronted you with that bill of sale? I'm really very sorry about that. Can you forgive me?"

Gus was astounded, "Oh, it was nothing, Sweetheart," he said.

From that time on, Trudi paid the same price as everyone else and was treated royally. Apparently the whole debacle embarrassed Gus, since he never mentioned it again. Trudi nursed her anger for a long time and, to this day, the memory of that hideous night still brings tears to her eyes.

❧

To deal with increased work stress, Trudi began to exercise. She had learned to play tennis after moving to Hinsdale and eventually joined a women's league. Even after her business expanded, Trudi wanted to continue to play. Each Monday, she rushed home from Chicago to make the league's early morning court time. Reluctant to have the ladies see her in her work clothes, Trudi parked the truck a couple of blocks away from the courts and changed into tennis clothes in the back of the truck.

The friends chatted while waiting for everyone to show up. None of them had any idea Trudi had been up most of the night and had driven there in a produce truck hidden around the corner. Anxious about her tight time schedule, she often pushed them to start play, yet no one ever suspected how much she struggled to maintain her concentration. When the match was over, she raced back to her truck, changed back into work clothes and made her deliveries.

One summer, her women's league received an invitation to play at an international tennis tournament in Mexico City. With few school sales during the summer, she decided to take the time off. Bill rearranged his flight schedule to care for the girls, and she was on her way.

Flying standby, Trudi felt relieved to get a seat on the earliest flight of the day. Arriving in Mexico City hours before everyone else, she had time for her favorite tourist activity, a bus tour around the city. Whenever she traveled to a new city anywhere in the world, she loved to take a public bus—the best way to see the city cheaply. Because buses drive a continuous loop, Trudi could stay on until they came back to where she started. Although her plan had worked successfully in many other countries, this time it backfired.

Outside the hotel, Trudi hopped on the first bus. The driver drove past Mexico City skyscrapers, past crowded apartment houses, then continued on country dirt roads past cacti and isolated houses. The bus became emptier and emptier until Trudi was the only passenger and the city a distant smudge on the horizon. Finally, the driver stopped next to a bus stop sign surrounded by barren ground and gestured to her to get out. With no idea where she was, Trudi said, "No way."

After arguing back and forth with her, the driver gave up and drove even farther into the country, this time stopping in the center of a little village, in front of a small adobe house. Chickens scratched in the bare dirt. "*Mi casa*," (my house) he told her as he stepped off the bus.

His whole family spilled out of the house, laughing and pointing at Trudi. She didn't budge from her seat. With her travel survival kit at hand, she knew she wouldn't starve. Two hours later, another driver arrived and walked into the house. Again everyone came out, laughing. Then the new driver climbed into the bus and began his route, which took Trudi back to the hotel.

She checked the route before her next foreign bus trip.

❦

After four years of working alone, juggling family and household responsibilities and squeezing in time for gardening, tennis and traveling, Trudi had worn herself out. The incessant energy it took to get up from her warm bed, drive a cold truck through the dangerous, dark Chicago streets and fight it out every night for the best product had become overwhelming.

Even her children were affected. Margo remembers being upset on the days when her mother didn't get home in time to get her ready for grade school. She didn't understand that Trudi had been up most of the night and was doing her best.

Bill knew how much his wife believed in her business and helped out at home—doing laundry, some cooking and braiding the girls' hair. But despite Bill's help and patience, Trudi felt her marriage starting to fall apart. In addition to being tired all the time, she rarely found time to cook a decent meal. Several times she even carried two briefcases to weddings. After greeting everyone at the conclusion of the ceremony, she would disappear into a back room to work. When she and Bill went to the opera or a concert, she opened up her briefcases while everyone else sipped champagne.

"*Das Ungetüm*"—the monster—was the name Trudi and her small staff of employees fondly called her business. Its incredible growth often overwhelmed her to the point that she had trouble figuring out whether she loved or hated her creation. Each month she thought, One more month and then I'll quit. Then some person or event—a happy customer, an enthusiastic sales rep, her new calculator—persuaded her to persevere for just one more month.

Trudi knew she had reached her limit. She silently begged, If You want me to continue this madness, send help. I need a partner, someone really special.

The pond garden

GARDEN TIP

The boulder garden

Garden Control

"I want to stand in my garden, turn 360° and be pleased. But that didn't happen early in my gardening career. I was a collector and stuffer with no regard for a plant's behavior. If it grew in the Chicago hardiness zone, I wanted it. I bought or traded first and then worried about where I might have another inch to stuff it. Some plants, like the Gooseneck Loosestrife (*Lysimachia clethroides*), could not be controlled and spread by rhizomes so fast that they soon consumed a large part of the garden. Others, like Purpletop Verbena (*Verbena bonariensis*), spread their seeds by the thousands and quickly went from beautiful plants to behaving like weeds. The total chaos in my garden was stressful. I almost felt ill. What was I going to do?"

Trudi realized she needed to control herself by pulling out the plants that annoyed her and becoming a displayer rather than a stuffer. She focused on creating larger groupings of plants that behaved well and pleased her. Though this change took a lot of discipline and time, the result is a magnificent, relaxing garden.

Whether the space set aside for a garden is large or small, the design principles remain the same. Select plants that please you, even without flowers present. Plant, for the most part, in large, nonlinear, noncircular groupings; nature doesn't plant in circles or straight lines. Here and there, place a single, especially eye-catching specimen, such as a Conifer or special Hosta.

Creeping Thyme *(Thymus praecox* 'Coccineus'*)*
Fleece Plant *(Persicaria polymorpha)* on friendship path

Help

Purple Coneflower *(Echinacea purpurea)*

One evening, two weeks after Trudi's plea, she heard a knock on her door. Not expecting anyone, she opened the door and saw a handsome young man standing there. "Mrs. Temple, my name is Greg Butler and I work for the Downer's Grove Park District. I've heard about what you're doing for the local schools with your business. I'd like to raise money for our Senior Center. Do you have time to talk to me tonight?"

"Sure," Trudi said, and immediately his avalanche of questions began. After talking nonstop for two hours, she suddenly realized what time it was. "Mr. Butler, you've got to leave. It's ten o'clock, my bedtime, and I have get up in three hours." Knowing he had more questions, Trudi added, "If you want to know more about my business, come to Chicago with me one night and I'll show you exactly what I'm doing."

Two nights later, Greg was standing next to Trudi's truck at 1:30 a.m. "I'm taking you up on your offer."

They talked all night as they made the rounds together, and Greg helped Trudi load the truck. After they finished at 6:30 that morning, Greg looked at her and said, "Lady, you work too hard."

"I know."

A few days later he called. "Trudi, I can't get you out of my mind. I love what you're doing, but you really are working too hard. I want to help. What can I do?"

"I don't think there's anything anyone can do for me."

"If you were to teach me what you do during the night in Chicago, maybe once a week I could do that for you. You could have a full night's sleep."

Trudi thought, This is unbelievable.

After his first trip, when she tried to pay him, he looked at her, surprised. "I would never do this for money; I do it because you need help."

Greg was a quick study and had a flare for business. Every Wednesday night for an entire year, he dressed in jeans and a shirt and came to Trudi's house to collect the papers. Using the guest bath as his locker room, he hung his suit and stashed his briefcase behind the door. Trudi slept through the night as he drove to Chicago, gathered the orders, loaded the truck and drove back to Hinsdale. After a quick shower, he stepped into his suit, grabbed his briefcase and went to work for the Park District.

※

To Trudi, he was like Superman without the cape or telephone booth.

One day Greg asked Trudi, "What's your gross?"

"I don't even know, Greg. I'm too busy to figure it out. All I know is that I have enough money to pay the bills and make mission donations. If you want to know for sure, take my books." He accepted her offer, brought back beautifully organized records and taught Trudi better accounting methods.

After a year, Greg said, "Trudi, I love doing this and I'm ready to do more." Delighted with his enthusiasm, Trudi gave him two nights a week. Greg still refused payment.

Occasionally, Greg stopped a truck and gave the driver five dollars to look inside. Greg studied the shelving and the way the truck was laid out. Then he and Trudi talked about how to implement those ideas. As spring turned to summer, refrigeration became an issue. At that time, all products were fresh; nothing was frozen.

"Trudi, you could get into trouble," Greg warned. "We need to figure out how to cool the meat in the truck and at the schools." Greg bought lumber to frame the inside of Trudi's truck and then stuffed insulation between the studs. They added dry ice to keep the meat cool.

Meanwhile, Greg, thinking creatively about ways to also keep the meat cold in school gyms, experimented with a compressor and set up a tent in his living room. He ran the compressor for weeks, trying to find a way to make it work at schools. Linda, Greg's patient wife, just laughed off the mess, telling Trudi, "He loves to solve problems." The tent idea never came to fruition; they kept meat cool at the sales by using more dry ice.

Greg, an athlete and very strong, loved the physical work that Trudi struggled with. Moreover, her motivation and passion was renewed when sharing the load with him. As an added benefit, Linda, Greg, Bill and Trudi became great friends.

Greg and Trudi shared a run one winter night when the wind chill hovered around twenty below. On the loading dock, Trudi had her wool hat pulled down over her forehead and her jacket collar turned up. The frigid wind stung their exposed skin. Knowing Trudi was chilled to the bone, Greg asked her, "Do you know somewhere we could get some hot soup?"

"I know just the place." They drove to the all-night diner a few blocks away, and Trudi ran in to get chicken soup. Back in the truck, she handed one giant Styrofoam™ container to Greg, wrapped icy hands around her steaming cup and took a big sip.

Without a word, Greg put the lid back on and set the cup down in the dashboard holder. Trudi asked, "Why aren't you drinking your soup?"

He quietly replied, "I can't handle the soup and drive at the same time."

Trudi finished hers, savoring every delicious swallow, forgetting about Greg's untouched cup. The next day she drove the same truck and found his cup, frozen solid with the lid popped off. Glancing into the cup, she recoiled in disgust when she saw the whole head of a chicken staring back at her. No wonder he didn't eat it, she thought.

Later on, Trudi asked Greg why he hadn't said anything to her. "Well, I thought about it, but you were enjoying that soup. I didn't have the heart to spoil it for you, but I couldn't drink it either."

❧

After two years of Greg's help, Trudi still felt exhausted. The years of driving into Chicago in the middle of the night, loading and unloading the truck and doing most of the bookwork left her without her usual stamina. Each evening her family saw how tired she was. Five minutes after Bill started reading in his soothing, gentle voice, her head drooped as she fell asleep.

Despite her fatigue, Trudi insisted on attending as many of Trudianne and Margo's after-school activities as possible. Margo, loving horses since she was a little girl, had become an expert equestrienne. Her classes and competitions often took them hours away from home. Trudi's solution was to buy a motor home. She could watch the class or do bookwork, but often she couldn't keep her eyes open and fell asleep. To watch Margo ride, she set an alarm clock.

When Trudi, forty-two years old, developed high blood pressure and an irregular heartbeat, her doctor prescribed Valium® and recommended she quit her job. Bill agreed. Trudi reluctantly told Greg her Benefit Marketing days were over, although she didn't tell him about her health problems.

Trudi and Greg

Greg said, "Oh, you can't quit, Trudi. It would be terrible."

"Greg, it's ruining me; it's going to kill me. I don't have to do this for a living. Bill is a fine provider."

"I know, but it's a great business and you have to continue. How can I talk you into this?"

"I need a partner," Trudi insisted, "but not a female partner. It's not a lady's job; I need a man."

Greg didn't answer. A few days later he phoned, "Trudi, would I do as your partner?"

Trudi couldn't have been happier. She knew Greg would be taking a big risk leaving his steady job for her business. He had just begun a career in public service and must have wondered if the two of them could succeed. "Greg, I can't imagine anyone else as my partner. If you consent, I'll give you half the business. I'll work with you as long as you need me, but you'll have to be the boss. Two bosses would be a disaster. You should take Benefit Marketing into the future."

On the momentous day in 1978 when they became partners, Trudi gave Greg a gold pocket watch with the inscription "*Es ist für immer.*" (It is forever.)

Over the next three years (1978–1981), they worked closely together as Greg continued to lighten Trudi's load, which resolved Trudi's health problems. With the business growing, both Greg and Trudi drove trucks into Chicago. Greg found a company that built specially insulated steel trucks. Their first real refrigerated truck was about thirty feet long with a stick shift. To drive it, they each needed a heavy-vehicle license.

Greg, though strong, strained to handle the clumsy truck at first. For Trudi, it felt like trying to steer a stegosaurus. Wearing sturdy boots to support her ankles for shifting, Trudi was petrified the first time she drove the monster into Chicago. She thought she should hang a sign from the back of the truck, "First time trucker; please be patient with me." She inched along in the right lane the entire way. When Trudi's truck finally rolled up to the loading dock, she asked for help to back the truck up. With plenty of practice, she finally came to terms with that behemoth.

Their business styles complemented each other. Greg, a talented, conservative businessman, carefully thought through details of a business plan before agreeing to it. Free-spirited Trudi generated ideas—some realistic, some not—while soaking in the bathtub. Whenever she revealed her latest brainstorm, Greg would roll his eyes and say, "Now, wait a minute, Trudi. Land that airplane." After some good-natured give and take, they'd agree—except for one rainy night in Chicago.

Greg usually loaded all the heavy items on one truck, and Trudi picked up the lighter things in the smaller truck. At South Water Market, they'd repack the two trucks and then make deliveries. That night, just as they began rearranging their loads, it started to pour. Trudi thought they could use umbrellas or even a tarp to keep the bread in her truck dry during the transfer to Greg's truck. Instead, Greg suggested backing the trucks up to each other. Trudi objected because his way blocked the road. Greg insisted his approach was easier and quicker, but Trudi was adamant about doing it her way and not inconveniencing other drivers. Soon she was shouting.

Greg stepped back and looked at her, amazed. "Trudi, are you hollering at me?"

Surprised at his calm tone, Trudi had to admit, "I guess I am."

"Let's never argue again," said Greg.

They never had another fight in all the years they worked together.

❧

Trudi did not take the girls to the markets until after she and Greg became partners. One Saturday morning before dawn, they drove into Chicago and explored. The girls were overwhelmed by the market and awed by kind words from so many rough men who had become Trudi's friends. Their morning ended with a picnic breakfast Trudi spread out on a loading dock at Randolph Street Market.

Trudi at the wheel

Margo and Trudianne remember another trip visiting South Water Street when a robbery unfolded in front of them. As two men grabbed a television and ran past their van, Trudi said calmly, "Look, they're stealing." Although it was nothing new for Trudi, the girls were horrified.

Benefit Marketing grew rapidly as they focused on raising funds for education. Trudi bought a small, combined office-warehouse, and slowly Greg delegated Trudi's jobs to others. Their next employee was Jim Huber, their first full-time truck driver. While he drove the big truck, Trudi could drive a car to the city to do the buying. Though she still had to get up at night, she found the work considerably less strenuous without wrestling with trucks. (Jim now manages the transportation department and remains Trudi's dear friend.) Hiring another secretary relieved Trudi of the burden of handing the billing and office work.

Once the business expanded beyond Illinois, they could no longer use the name, Benefit Marketing. Someone else had registered that name and wouldn't relinquish it without charging an exorbitant fee. Greg suggested a new name, "Market Day," and Trudi loved it.

By 1981, Greg needed an escape valve, a restful spot away from work pressures. He asked Trudi to help him look for a cottage. Trudi was also devouring the real-estate pages—due to her father's generosity. While she lived in Germany, he had rarely given her gifts other than half her bike; gift giving was her mother's province. But once Trudi left Germany, her father had given her money for a vacation, bought her a coat and an entire set of prized Meissen china.

On one of her visits to Germany, Trudi confessed how much she missed the family farm. Her father astounded Trudi by responding, "Just go and buy yourself a farm. I'll give you the money." During the search for Greg's cottage, she found a small farm in northern Illinois and used her father's gift as the down payment.

As she looked forward to the joy of springtime gardening, Trudi realized she could use her new farm to solve her asparagus dilemma. Each spring, Trudi's customers wanted asparagus. Since the market sold it at such a high price, Trudi couldn't afford to add it without sacrificing variety in her produce box. One day she came up with the perfect solution: she would grow her own asparagus on her new farm. Instead of buying costly seedlings, Trudi bought fifty pounds of asparagus seed and then borrowed a tractor and corn planter from a neighbor. After farmer Henry Thomforda plowed a one-acre field, they planted the asparagus seeds together.

Several weeks later, Trudi drove to the farm, expecting to see evenly spaced baby asparagus plants. Instead, she was horrified to see the field looking like a massive green lawn. Then she realized what had happened. Fifty pounds of asparagus seeds, way too much for one acre, had poured out onto the field through the overly large corn-planter holes.

Overwhelmed when she looked at those little plants, Trudi decided to ignore them until the following spring. By then, her work was so draining it became hard to find the energy for anything else. Yet, if she wanted to salvage any future asparagus, she knew those baby plants had to be transplanted.

Five farm hands and Henry helped Trudi plow twenty additional acres and carefully dig up the plants. As they started planting them, one by one, she began worrying about all those precious bare-rooted plants drying out in the sun. If planting them took too long, they'd all die. She told her helpers, "Just throw them in—right side up, upside down; doesn't matter."

They planted twenty acres in three days. When they were done, Trudi said to Henry, "You may call me 'Fritz' if these come up."

They all came up, but there's a four-year wait until the first harvest. When the asparagus finally matured, the business had outgrown the field and Trudi didn't have enough for all the customers.

After all that time and effort, she never sold the farm's bountiful asparagus crop to Market Day. Without much demand for U-pick asparagus in farm country, Trudi made oceans of asparagus soup, froze other asparagus dishes and gifted her family and friends with the rest.

※

There is no time to be sick when you're a new farmer, a business owner, a wife and mother. On the way to Trudianne's flute lesson in Naperville, thirty minutes away from home, Trudi felt a sharp pain in her abdomen. Stopping at the Market Day office for a quick glass of water, she drove on, determined Trudianne wouldn't miss her lesson.

When they arrived in Naperville, Trudi told Trudianne not to tell anyone she had a tummy ache. Trudianne agreed and went in for her lesson. Alone in the van, Trudi became ill, vomiting and groaning with severe pain. She couldn't think straight, much less imagine driving home.

Suddenly Bill opened the van door. Trudianne, smart enough to know something was seriously wrong, had called her dad. He took one look at Trudi's pale, sweaty face and drove straight to the hospital.

A kidney stone was diagnosed, and noninvasive treatment failed. After Trudi had several more painful attacks that fall, the doctor advised surgery. Trudi refused to consider taking weeks off from Market Day to recover. After the busy holiday season, she canceled the long-delayed surgery to go on a family ski trip.

Several days later, as the chair lift bumped and swayed on its way to the top of the Colorado mountain, Trudi's heart sank. She felt the dreaded pain begin to build. But, by the time she skied off the lift, the pain had vanished and she never had another attack.

During that same year, Greg told Trudi she could stay home if she found a produce buyer. She couldn't believe it. The time had finally come. She immediately thought of Ed Peck, the mushroom salesman, and presented her plan. "Ed, I've got a great opportunity for you. If you're ready for a new challenge, you could become the Market Day produce buyer." He agreed. To show her enthusiasm and seal the agreement, Trudi gave him her precious calculator, the numbers long worn off. He treasured that gift and became one of their most talented and successful employees, dedicated to Market Day.

Market Day Funds at Work

The money Market Day distributes to schools has been used in many creative ways. One school bought buses; another established an entire computer lab. Some schools have funded Thanksgiving boxes for the needy. Others have paid for field trips, books, playground equipment and band instruments.

Elephant Ears *(Colocasia esculenta* 'Black Magic'*)*
Ornamental Cabbage *(Brassica oleracea)* with railroad wagon

GARDEN TIP

Think Big

"Don't dream small dreams," is a guiding principle of Trudi's life, exemplified by her Market Day career, her garden, even her kitchen. "Everything, from my planter boxes to the boulders for my rock garden to the teacups in my kitchen, has to be large," she insists. "This principle even applies to the number of bulbs I plant in one hole—never six or nine; a minimum of twenty-five is my rule. Every time I violate the principle of big, I regret it."

More than one hundred tons of large Wisconsin limestone boulders have been placed in her garden. They form a path through her front garden, the steps leading into the rotunda garden and the foundation for her boulder garden and pond. She likes to use natural boulders rather than man-made stone products, because their shapes blend in better with her garden design.

Trudi's largest planter box is the railroad luggage cart in the far back corner of her yard. A box made of treated wood was built on top of the cart, disguised with old barn wood and filled with aged horse manure. This wagon, situated in a mostly shaded area, provides a stunning display for Fuschias, Ferns, Croton and Impatiens and serves as an ideal summerhouse for many of her house plants.

The pond garden

The backyard

PART FOUR

IN THE GARDEN

Reproduction grape cart
Variegated Spider Plant *(Chlorophytum comosum* 'Vittatum'*)*
Dragon Wing Begonia *(B. x hybrida* 'Dragon Wing'*)*
Emerald Fern *(Asparagus densiflorus* 'Sprengeri'*)*
Iboza *(I. riparia)*

Family Ties

Oriental Poppy
(Papaver orientale 'Turkenlouis')

With Ed Peck trained, abruptly Trudi found herself staying home. Although she remained on the Board of Directors, her Market Day years of hyperactivity—years in orbit, constantly thinking, organizing, meeting deadlines—were over. Even though Trudi couldn't have been more overjoyed with the idea of total freedom, at forty-six she was still full of energy, too young to leave the working world.

Suffering from workaholic withdrawal, she sank into depression—unable to sleep, without an appetite and not wanting to do anything around the house. Trudi often wondered why she should bother to get dressed. Because Bill's job and his many volunteer commitments made his free time limited, she couldn't count on him to fill her time.

Her doctor again prescribed Valium®, telling Trudi to stop clenching her hands and to start singing songs. But prescription drugs and folk songs didn't save her; her garden did. She channeled all that Market Day vigor into transforming her yard. After two weeks, she stopped the Valium® and sat up half the night making sketches of possible garden designs.

First, Trudi had to fight the ongoing family battle of the titans: Bill vs. Trudi, the case of his lawn vs. her expanding gardens. Bill wouldn't relent from his protective stance on his lawn. Trudi moans, "I don't know what it is about American men and their lawns!"

Their first compromise established a mulch border between the flower beds and the lawn, but this didn't satisfy Trudi. Whenever she took her spade and edged along the border, another two inches to two feet of lawn disappeared, and more garden appeared.

One day Bill glanced out the bedroom window and caught her at it. He opened the window and called out, "Trudi, there won't be any lawn left! You have to stop that. We need to put in a permanent edging, so we'll know who owns what."

They dragged out the hoses to mark the new boundary lines between their warring provinces. Bill moved the hoses in to save his precious lawn, and then Trudi moved them out to gain more garden space. They simply couldn't agree.

Bill's Philanthropic Work

When Bill wasn't working, his life revolved around family and service to others. As a sky angel, he flew needy people to hospitals at no cost. He volunteered in the community as a school board member, lay preacher and treasurer for their church and a speaker on ethics in the workplace.

Passionately involved in Rotary, Bill became known for promoting the use of solar ovens—to save trees from being cut down to fuel woodstoves. Rotary International adopted this initiative, now called the Temple Solar Oven Project, successful all over the world.

Trudi admired his attitude as a servant and adopted his softer, more patient approach. She learned to temper her enthusiasm—not to say, "You must . . ." but to suggest, "You might like to try . . ." She asked, "What do you think of . . . ?" instead of stating, "I think . . ."

Determined to have more real estate, Trudi devised a scheme. "OK, Bill. You win. Just lay it out exactly the way you want it." Meanwhile she called Steve, a local landscaper, and asked him to come the day Bill was leaving for his next three-day trip. Before Bill returned, Steve and Trudi made garden beds exactly to her specifications—with foot-high rock edging cemented into place.

When Bill came home, he was floored to see his lawn had shrunk again. He knew they hadn't laid out the borders like that. Without getting angry, Bill firmly extracted Trudi's promise to never, ever garden in front of that new border.

Although Trudi won the lawn battle, the garden beds were now too large. She decided to break them up with steps, boulders and berms to create different levels. Over a ten-year period, a dozen garden rooms blossomed, each developing into a restful sanctuary. Arranging this giant bouquet of gardens became Trudi's therapy and her saving grace.

❧

Even though Trudi kept busy with her new gardening projects, over the next few years several family events created personal turmoil. Both of her girls left home within two years. Trudianne left first to begin college at Bucknell University in Pennsylvania in 1983, a year after Trudi retired from her full-time Market Day role.

Margo had a bedroom full of blue ribbons and grand prize awards—tribute to her horseback-riding passion. Two years after Trudianne left for Bucknell, Margo decided to go to The Kent School in Connecticut for her last two years of high school. She loved the expert riding instruction and outstanding academics there. After graduation, she also went to Bucknell. By then, Trudianne, who had learned to fly when she was sixteen, had graduated and was commissioned in the Air Force. Although Trudi grieved when the girls left home, this happy stage in their lives had been expected.

The other family event during this time took Trudi by surprise and broke her heart. In 1984, her father had a series of strokes. Unable to walk or live independently any longer, he was miserable. Trudi flew to Germany to visit him in the nursing home, and he begged her to bring him his pistol. When she told him, "No way," he sighed and asked her to buy him a big five-pound box of his favorite chocolates before she left. She certainly could grant that request and brought him a beautiful box of Swiss chocolates the night before her departure. Her father, unusually talkative that night, told Trudi story after story, including the details of his POW experience.

Two hours after Trudi arrived home, the phone rang; she heard the shocking news that her beloved father was dead. He had rapidly eaten the entire box of chocolates, surmising correctly that eating so much candy in his weakened condition would cause his blood sugar to soar and then crash. He died of insulin shock.

Trudi immediately flew back to Germany. Distraught, she sobbed to Rudi, "I killed my father."

"Don't be ridiculous!" Rudi folded his travel-worn, red-eyed sister into his arms. "He knew exactly what he was doing."

Trudi comments, "My sadness over his death persists to this day because of all the years I didn't appreciate his kindness, support and tremendous strength of character. Missing all those opportunities to be close to my father during my preteen and teen years, I made myself miserable and was the loser."

❧

Another family crisis consumed Trudi in 1988. The day before Mother's Day, Margo called from college and left a message that she was sick and had gone to the local hospital. They had sent her back to the dorm with a diagnosis of rheumatic fever.

> Realizing the gravity of Margo's illness, he promised to find her...

Frantic at hearing that message, Trudi and Bill wondered how the doctor could possibly have allowed her to leave the hospital. When Trudi called Margo, there was no answer. Panicking, she called a family friend, Dr. Mowad, a neurologist from Danville, Pennsylvania, and explained the situation. Realizing the gravity of Margo's illness, he promised to find her, but kindly didn't tell Trudi about a local student who had just died of bacterial meningitis.

Dr. Mowad called the dorm and let the phone ring and ring until finally Margo answered. She had been lying on her bed, drifting in and out of consciousness. Margo, sounding slightly incoherent, told Dr. Mowad about her rash. Alarmed, he told her to find someone in the dorm to drive her immediately to Geisinger Medical Center, thirty minutes away.

Dr. Mowad went straight to Geisinger, rounded up a team of doctors and waited for Margo. When she hadn't arrived after forty-five minutes, he wisely called the local hospital and discovered Margo back in their emergency room, already delirious. He ordered the doctors to pump her full of penicillin, put her in an ambulance and rush her to Geisinger.

By the time the ambulance arrived, Margo was unconscious. Later that night, Dr. Mowad called to tell Trudi and Bill their daughter had bacterial meningitis and they should fly out immediately. With Margo in critical condition, the Air Force granted emergency leave to Trudianne, who was stationed in Florida.

When Bill and Trudi arrived, Margo had been placed in isolation. Seeing her unresponsive and curled up in a fetal position, they were consumed with fear. Wearing gowns and masks, her family stayed by her bed and prayed for the next two days. She didn't move or respond.

On the third day, Trudi decided to call Margo's friend in California to cancel her upcoming visit. She picked up Margo's purse on the bedside table and rummaged around in it, looking for the friend's phone number. Suddenly Margo said, "Whatcha looking for, Mom?" What a glorious feeling it was for her family to hear her voice.

Eleven days later, Trudi and Bill took Margo home to begin her recuperation. Over the next few years, despite a paralyzed left arm, impaired vision and limited short-term memory, she recovered fully, although she didn't get straight A's again until the end of her senior year.

Bill and Trudi, 1987

Trudianne Temple

As Trudi helped Margo through her recovery, she had time to face a difficult issue—her citizenship. Even though she had felt like an American for nearly thirty years, she had yet to become a citizen. Her father had expressed extremely strong feelings about her remaining a German citizen. Each visit, the first thing he'd ask was, "Are you still a German?"

After his death, Trudi felt disloyal thinking about it. Nine years later, finally geared up psychologically, she spent hours studying two hundred years of American history and government. By the time she took the citizenship test in 1993, she felt like an expert. Chagrined, Trudi discovered the test was easy enough for a kindergartener, with questions such as "What are the colors of the American flag?"

After Trudi was sworn in as a new American citizen, her gardening friend, Kellie O'Brien, threw a big surprise party for her. Red, white and blue gifts surrounded a cake decorated with tiny American flags. So many people celebrated with Trudi she felt inspired to give a speech. When she began with, "My fellow Americans . . . ," everyone applauded.

Trudi welcomed the next family event—Margo's wedding. Bill had introduced Alex, a pilot from the Netherlands, to Margo in 1991. They became friends instantly and dated over the next three years.

Trudi's garden was the site of the wedding in May 1994. When Rudi sent one thousand white Lisianthus from his flower business in Germany, Trudi joyfully wove them into the pergola and added them to the table centerpieces at the reception.

On the day of the wedding, Bill proudly escorted radiant Margo past the guests lining the grassy path where Alex waited under the arch.

Robert Kelly Studio

Primrose *(Primula vulgaris)*

Near the front door

GARDEN TIP

Bigleaf Hydrangea *(H. machrophylla 'Nikko Blue')*

Painting with Color

During the 1991 Gulf War, with Trudianne still serving in the military, Trudi began flying the flag every day. When she looked around at her pastel garden, she realized there were no red flowers to complement the flag. To solve that problem, she added red to her window boxes with Ivy Geraniums and Begonias. They delighted her so much she started planting swaths of red flowers throughout her yard. Trudi even planted a spectacular monochromatic red garden at Trudianne's house.

Ten years later, vibrant red, orange and purple flowers create a powerful impact in Trudi's garden.

Canna Lily *(Canna edulis 'Pretoria')*

Peony *(Paeonia 'America')*
Doublefile Viburnum *(V. plicatum* var. *tomentosum 'Shasta')*

Common Bugle *(Ajuga reptans)*
Dwarf Larkspur *(Delphinium tricorne)*
Climbing Hydrangea *(H. anomala petiolaris)* foliage

155

Walkway to the lower sky garden
Astilbe *(Astilbe arendsii* 'Peach Blossom'*)*
Astilbe *(A. arendsii* 'White Gloria'*)*

White Water Lily *(Nymphaea occidentalis 'Alba')*

Remembrance

Before bedtime, Trudi and Bill had a routine of playing cards. Gin rummy was their favorite. One tranquil evening in October 1997, Bill asked, "Want to play a round of cards?"

"Sure, I'd love to."

"Great, first let me finish paying some bills."

"Fine. I'll go upstairs and read for a while." Trudi climbed into bed and began reading while she waited. Soon her eyes grew heavy, and the book slipped out of her hand. At midnight, she woke up and reached for Bill before even opening her eyes. His side of the bed was cool, empty. She had a terrible premonition. He never stayed up this late. She called out for him. Why wasn't he answering? She ran down the stairs and called again. Silence.

The moment she saw him, Trudi knew. The scene would be indelibly etched in her mind—the quiet room, the lamp still on, his body motionless. "Oh, Bill, Bill," she cried, as she ran to him and hugged him close. There was no response; he felt cold. She grabbed the phone, dialed 911 and ran outside, screaming for help.

She saw the flashing lights of the police car pulling into the driveway, heard the siren of the approaching ambulance, knew the paramedics had rushed past her.

Her wait was short. The paramedics walked back outside to tell her there was nothing that they could do. She called Margo and Alex. Alex answered the phone. From her side of the bed, Margo heard screaming and knew what had happened without Alex saying a word.

Bill was gone.

Later, the doctor told Trudi that even if she had been standing right next to him, there was nothing she could have done to help Bill survive such a massive heart attack.

Trudi, Margo and Alex could comfort each other, but how to tell Trudianne? Trudi couldn't just call her in Kentucky and tell her about her dad. Alex, Margo and Trudi slept no more that night.

Instead they drove to Trudianne's house—a nightmarish eight-hour trip. She wasn't there when they arrived, so they waited, occupying their time by cleaning up the garden.

Late that afternoon, Trudianne, a USAF C-130 Hercules navigator, bounced in from a trip. "What are you guys doing here?" she asked cheerfully. Trudi couldn't speak the words; Margo looked at her and Trudianne knew. She was devastated and inconsolable, as they all were.

During Bill's funeral, Trudi encouraged the girls not to look at him in his casket. She wanted them to remember their dad smiling and happy. Numb with shock, they clung to each other over the next few weeks. Trudianne's Air Force commitment had expired, and she quickly decided to give up her military career and return home to Illinois to be close to her mother.

Trudi's whole life turned upside down. She knew she could fix most things through hard work, money or creativity. Not this. She couldn't bring Bill back, a truth almost impossible to accept. She agonized because he had died without her at his side. Often, at suppertime, when Bill and Trudi would have been eating together, she wept without warning. They would never share growing old together and watching their grandchildren grow up.

Although others thought Trudi was brave—and she did try to be strong for the girls—her entire personality seemed to have changed. Her positive, happy attitude vanished. Collecting all her favorite pictures, she created a Bill Memorial Wall in the family room. Every time Trudi walked by, sadness overwhelmed her. She managed the lonely evenings by going to bed right after supper, watching C-Span and reading until sleep overtook her.

> After midnight that day was over . . . . I decided to live for today.

Trudi adopted a new philosophy: "After midnight, that day was over. It became yesterday. Tomorrow was unknown, so I decided to live for today."

Friends rallied around Trudi, each offering invaluable support. Bill Gothard, her neighbor and founder of the Institute in Basic Life Principles, knew Bill had done many jobs around the house. Mr. Gothard sent Institute helpers to mow the lawn, clean the gutters and make repairs. His kindness gave Trudi enormous peace of mind.

The first Christmas season after Bill died, Trudi didn't decorate inside or outside the house. When a thoughtful friend, J. R. Phillips of Phillips Flowers, drove down the street and saw how sad the house looked, he hung a gorgeous wreath on the front door, without saying a word to her.

When Trudi found herself missing Bill so intensely she again became depressed. She tried to focus on the things he had done that annoyed her. For example, when she'd ask him if he was hungry, he'd look at his watch. If it was noon, he was hungry, but if it was eleven forty-five, "No, not hungry." Trudi always enjoyed anytime, adventurous eating, but he wanted meat, potatoes and vegetables served on time. Now, Trudi could eat a hodgepodge any time of the day or night and no one would comment—chips and a salad for breakfast, cheese and hot chocolate for dinner. And she could do anything in her garden without his objections.

However, thinking of their differences and the choices she could now make on her own didn't help. Making choices was an empty freedom compared to sharing her life with Bill.

In January, about three months after Bill died, Trudi was flustered by an odd event when she listened to her answering machine messages. Instead of a message from one of the girls or a friend, there was a message from Bill. "Just checking in—no news. All is well." Shocked, she wondered if she had pushed a button to replay an old message, but couldn't find it and never heard it again. Nevertheless, his voice and the idea that Bill might have sent her a message comforted her.

> Making choices was an empty freedom compared to sharing her life with Bill.

Trudi talked to him and felt his presence constantly. Time after time she asked him for help and suddenly help appeared. Bill became the family's "saint of lost items." The first time he helped her was when she searched unsuccessfully for a special photograph of him in his files. Finally, totally frustrated, she thought, *Bill, where is that picture?* When she checked the files again, she found the picture—in the first file she opened.

Another time, Trudi couldn't find her tennis shoes and asked Bill, "Where are my tennis shoes?" Just then Trudianne called and added, at the end of the conversation, "By the way, Mom, I borrowed your tennis shoes and forgot to return them."

More recently, Trudianne was packing for a trip and looking for her glasses. Running out of time and frantic, she phoned her mom, who suggested, "Did you ask Daddy?"

"Yes and he didn't help me," she grumbled.

Trudi drove over to Trudianne's house and pleaded, "Bill, come on. Help us out." She walked over to the couch, moved one pillow and uncovered the glasses.

Hawaiian Rose *(Hibiscus sinensis* 'Maiden's Blush'*)*
Trudi placed this perfect blossom on Bill's grave.

Mail—The 3D Method

Trudi devised a 3D method for dealing with the onslaught of mail she receives daily. She "Dumps it, Delegates it or Does it." She takes the mail directly to her wastebasket and dumps the junk mail. (Wastepaper ends up in a "Trudi pit.") Some of the business mail can be delegated to someone at Market Day. The mail requiring her attention goes to her desk, where it's immediately sorted into the cubbies labeled for bills, credit card receipts, personal correspondence and receivables.

Gene Garcia at the farm

Once spring arrived, gardening became Trudi's salvation. Her garden world distracted her so she didn't focus as much on Bill. She did make sure to decorate his gravesite, just a short walk from her garden, with her loveliest flowers.

The grieving process did not ease after the first year. The second year without Bill seemed even more painful than the first, with almost anything triggering her sadness. On one of her walks, she walked along a lake Bill loved and composed a poem about missing him. It began:

I see the lake you loved

Its color like wet slate

I hear the bullfrog's call

He's calling for his mate.

That fall, a major plumbing problem turned into a godsend. Bill Gothard came to the rescue again after Trudi had been given a sky-high quote of six thousand dollars to dig up the garden and repair the pipes. He sent over his repairman, Gene Garcia, who fixed the problem without ruining the garden and charged nothing.

Trudi told Gene she wished she could clone him to help her on the farm. He spoke with Bill Gothard, who graciously responded, "If Trudi needs you, we can work this out." Gene, a talented carpenter and handyman, began working for Trudi. His entire family became dear friends.

Trudi, feeling out of control, worried about falling behind and not getting everything done. For solace, she turned to organizing. At least she could control putting her life in order. In the middle of the night, Trudi remembered a sock she had found in the wrong drawer the day before and ended up reorganizing the entire closet.

Over the next few months, she organized socks, pencils, and the garage, before starting in on Bill's things. After packing up all the precious mementos her children or future grandchildren might want, Trudi gave everything else away. She had begun a new chapter in her life.

February brought the exciting news of Margo's pregnancy. Thrilled at the thought of becoming an *Oma* (grandmother), Trudi dreamed about the future. She knew she would drop everything to help when Margo called.

Kendall and "*Omi*"

After a long nine months, the entire family rejoiced when Margo and Alex had Kendall, a healthy baby girl, in August 1999. Although immersed in baby care, Margo missed sharing the joys and challenges of her new baby with her dad. She often said, "I can't believe he's not here to see her."

Trudianne had almost given up searching for a true passion in her life. Her mom had her garden and her sister had her family. Although Trudianne's family recognized her musical talents, she had dismissed her own abilities. When she was on duty in northern Scotland, she heard the magical sound of fine Highland bagpiping. Then, the year her father died, she began playing the bagpipes and soon fell in love with piping. The precision and challenge of an instrument that could never be truly mastered appealed to her organized mind. At last she had found a worthy goal and her life's work.

On the social front, the dating scene frustrated Trudianne until she met Adrian, a well-known bagpiper from Scotland, at a master class. Trudianne always sat in the chair next to the electrical outlet, but this day Adrian chanced to sit in it. She asked him to move, and they began to chat. Soon the conversation turned into a whirlwind courtship.

Trudi was thrilled to prepare for another garden wedding in August 2000. This time Kendall, dressed in a long purple dress and wearing a circlet of flowers, toddled through the garden, holding Margo's hand and throwing rose petals. Adrian's father played the bagpipes as Trudianne walked alone through the garden to Adrian.

Trudi placed an empty chair beside her in remembrance of Bill.

Trudianne's wedding

Thornapple *(Datura metel* 'Alba'*)*

GARDEN TIP

The White Garden

Trudi's white garden room was her greatest design challenge. Many white flowers are actually slightly off-white, tinged with yellow, pink or blue. They are not welcome in a pure white garden. Hibiscus *(Hibiscus syriaca* 'Diana'), Brazilian Jasmine *(Mandevilla sanderi)*, Columbine *(Aquilegia hybrida)* and Thornapple *(Datura metel* 'Alba')* star in this garden.

At the far end of her white garden, a large metal pergola arches over to her dance floor garden. Every fall, it's covered with the tiny white flowers of Sweet Autumn Clematis *(C. paniculata* 'Sweet Autumn'). In the evening, when light fades, Trudi enjoys sitting on a bench and looking across the lawn at her white garden, glowing in the sweet night air.

Clematis *(C. paniculata* 'Sweet Autumn')*

Steps to the rotunda garden

A Brand-New Day

Camas *(Camassia quamash)*

Recently Trudi drove alone from Arizona to Chicago, enjoying her search for unusual plants to take back to her garden. She heard something on the radio that immediately captivated her:

"We are not born a winner.

We are not born a loser.

We are born a chooser."

Unknown

More than two years after Bill's death, Trudi finally took down his Memorial Wall because it was too upsetting. Choosing to stop being miserable, Trudi was determined to recreate a happy life and explore new horizons. As she healed, a myriad of activities, planned and unplanned, kept her busy.

Her next adventure was unexpected. Trudianne coaxed her mother out of the garden on a sunny day and drove her to Wisconsin, not telling Trudi where they were going. Trudi was puzzled until she saw the hang gliders in the field. Trudianne, who had been taking hang-gliding lessons, said enthusiastically, "Mom, you've got to experience this. Up in the sky you're as close to being free as you can get. It's so beautiful and peaceful up there."

True to form, Trudi thought, Why not?

A small airplane took off, towed the glider higher and higher and then released it. Flying in tandem with the instructor, Trudi soared over cornfields, rivers and Monopoly®-small houses. She watched the clouds shadowing the landscape, savoring every minute. Trudianne's airborne gift to her mom turned out to be an unforgettable thrill.

As Trudi landed, she threw out her arms, proclaiming to the universe, "This is great; what can we do next?" She realized at that moment that she had a lot of living to do.

Market Day Expands

Once Market Day had expanded into the Midwest, the East and the South, fresh foods were no longer practical; instead, Trudi and Greg introduced a variety of specialty frozen and packaged foods. Their customer base grew and supported Market Day's unique concept of raising funds for schools through the sale of high-quality food.

In June 2000, Greg and Trudi won an Ernst & Young Regional Entrepreneur of the Year award, an honor for them and all the Market Day employees across the country. With renewed enthusiasm, they tackled a new venture, their first Market Day retail store. That September, Greg and Trudi presided at the store's grand opening in the Chicago suburb of Itasca.

Laurie Bohlke

Trudi and Greg at retail store grand opening

In her sixties, Trudi continues to test her limits. One December, as she explored a new path in the woods, she spied an architectural wonder that had fascinated her all her life—a perfect paper wasp nest, nestled high in a Poplar Tree. She stopped and asked herself, "Who could I talk into climbing up that tree?" With no one around, Trudi had to rely on herself. Knowing hives were empty during the winter, she climbed up into the tree and made herself comfortable on a limb. She reached into the pocket of her jeans and pulled out her pocketknife. Trudi patiently whacked and whittled away at that branch until she could break it off. Holding the branch with the fragile nest in one hand, she carefully climbed back down and triumphantly walked home, delighted with herself and her prize.

Now that Trudi is less involved with Market Day, she finds time for other adventures. One of her current projects involves turning her farm into an arboretum. She travels around the country to find unusual trees and shrubs. Trudi will feature conifers with their striking four-season color and texture. She has already attacked the daunting issue of moving these new trees with large root balls.

Driving along a country road one day, she stopped and spoke to a road crew. Admiring their backhoe, she asked them where to buy one. Trudi had been toying with the idea of purchasing a backhoe for the farm. She and Gene then took their advice and traveled to central Illinois to an auction of used road equipment. After climbing over the massive machines, Trudi successfully bid on a used backhoe, which has become a hard worker at her farm.

❧

In quiet moments, Trudi takes time to be more reflective about what's truly important to her. Despite a lifetime of generous service to others, she remembers times in her life when she was guilty of offending and disappointing people. She still chides herself over an incident that occurred more than twenty years ago. At five one morning, Trudi began a seventeen-hour drive to Connecticut to visit Margo. She wore her favorite grey slacks, the ones that showed no dirt and didn't wrinkle—perfect for traveling. Before leaving town, she stopped to fill up the gas tank. As she waited in line to pay, a well-dressed man walked up behind her and stumbled, spilling his entire cup of hot coffee all over Trudi's slacks. Trudi's reaction is crystal clear in her memory.

"If I had been gracious or said nothing, I'm sure that he would have apologized and all would have been fine. Instead, I turned on him, 'Why don't you drink your d---- coffee at home instead of pouring it all over me?' Of course, he snapped back at me. We traded insults and nearly started a fistfight."

Trudi and her grandchildren, Kendall and Parker

Margo with Parker, Avery and Kendall

"Then I had to waste time going home to change clothes. All the way to Connecticut I was fuming, thinking of juicier, more cutting insults. Before I knew it, I was there and still furious. I hadn't enjoyed the trip at all—hadn't noticed any of the natural beauty of the countryside. I just knew the coffee man told everyone in his office that he had just met the worst witch."

"I scolded myself, 'What a waste of time and energy! You had the opportunity to make a friend and instead you made an enemy. That poor man hadn't meant to spill his coffee on you. It was just an accident.' I vowed then and there that I'd never do anything like that again. Anyone can get mad and hold a grudge. It's much better to forgive the other person and to choose to stay above the ugliness and nastiness. It's so much more fun to plant good things and touch people's lives in a positive way. Attitude makes you successful. Rather than looking for opportunity for yourself, find ways to help other people be successful. We each have that choice."

❦

Trudi's number-one priority is still her family. Trudianne and Adrian live just down the street; Margo and Alex now have three children: Kendall, Parker and Avery. One of Trudi's great joys is having her grandchildren stay with her overnight at the farm. Kendall loves the chickens. She eagerly collects eggs from the coop and tells each bird, as her *Omi* taught her, "Thank you, chicken." The minute she walks in the house, she asks for her eggs to be cooked.

Beyond cooking for grandchildren, Trudi uses her kitchen to show her love for her friends and family. They often take away a home-cooked treat—perhaps her special carrot cake. The story of this recipe begins with Trudi's philosophy of recycling everything, not wasting anything.

Trudi learned to love homemade juice as a child. Her mother made all kinds, depending on what was harvested at the farm. Now, Trudi uses an electric juicer year-round. In the late fall, after Trudi puts her vegetable garden to bed for another season, she harvests carrots and makes carrot juice. This process creates a mountain of leftover carrot pulp—powdery-dry, bright orange shavings that Trudi wouldn't dream of wasting. She uses the pulp to make carrot soup—so much carrot soup that it became breakfast, lunch and dinner. Trudi was desperate for carrot pulp rescue.

Sharing her carrot woes with Gregory Mondroski, her sweet-toothed dentist, led to the solution. "How about making carrot cake?" he asked.

Trudi had always disliked overly sweet carrot cake and wondered if she could create a Trudi version instead. On a mission, she studied her cookbooks and experimented. When she combined her

Bittersweet *(Celastrus orbiculatus)*

Trudi's Special Cranberry-Carrot Cake

4 c. walnut pieces, finely ground

4 c. all purpose flour

4 t. baking soda

2 t. baking powder

4 t. cinnamon

1 t. ground cloves

1 t. ground ginger

1 t. salt

3 c. sugar

1 c. raisins

8 eggs, slightly beaten

1 T. vanilla

1 c. milk, whole or skim

2 c. vegetable oil

3 pounds carrots (15 large), peeled

4 c. fresh or frozen cranberries

1/2 c. fresh lemon juice or lemon juice from concentrate

1 pound confectioner's sugar

1. In a large bowl, stir all dry ingredients together, ground walnuts through raisins. Add eggs, vanilla, milk and oil. Mix well.

2. Make carrot juice from carrots using an electric juicer. Set the juice aside to drink later. Add 4 cups of the leftover dry carrot pulp to the batter. Mix thoroughly.

3. Fold in cranberries.

4. Grease 5 medium (8x4) loaf pans. Divide the batter evenly among the 5 pans. Bake in preheated 375° oven for at least 1 hour, until toothpick in center comes out dry.

5. While cake is baking, make glaze by mixing together lemon juice and sugar.

6. Remove cakes from oven. Cool in pan for 20 minutes. Remove from pans. Place cakes on plate and immediately brush glaze over top and sides.

Makes 5 medium loaves. This cake freezes well. You can also substitute 6 muffin tins for 1 loaf pan. Bake the muffins for at least 30 minutes. Use a toothpick to check that the muffins are done.

favorite spices—ginger, cinnamon and cloves—and then added walnuts and cranberries, she created a winner.

The cakes flew out of her kitchen as family and friends devoured them. Alex, Trudi's son-in-law, was puzzled when she asked him how he'd liked the cake she'd sent home with Margo. "What cake?" he asked, only to discover that Margo and little Kendall had eaten the whole thing in the car coming home.

Trudi has refused repeated requests for the recipe because she wanted to offer it as a gift to all the readers of this book.

❧

During September and October, Trudi devotes the majority of her time preparing for "Autumn Drive" at her farm. On the third weekend of October, farms along a two-mile stretch of road sell crafts, baked goods, pumpkins, apples, antiques and garage sale treasures. It's a family endeavor; Trudi, Margo, Alex, Trudianne and Adrian share the work. Trudi also creates a plethora of dried flower arrangements and decorates for the festivities.

At the farm

Winter is a more tranquil time for Trudi. "Last December, I went to the farm early one morning. It was about thirty degrees, a beautiful clear day. I pruned my raspberries, cleaned out the barn, let the chickens out, and found two fresh eggs. For lunch I ate the eggs, bread and some homemade yogurt my friend, Audrey, had made. I felt happy all day working around the farm and dreaming —making things orderly and beautiful. Just the chickens, two cats and me. Everything was fine. I was at peace."

What keeps Trudi going long after others have slowed down? She explains, "I have to have a dream, something that excites me. I'm always designing businesses in my mind and get so fired up thinking about what I could do. At the farm, I could have a small cut-flower business or an intimate soup restaurant featuring my favorite family recipes, but some of these ideas are just not feasible. There are only twenty-four hours in a day. What I like best is making things beautiful. When I get up in the morning, I think, this is a brand-new day. I'm ready to create, ready to make people smile."

> I have to have a dream, something that excites me.

APPENDIX

The friendship path

Acknowledgments

Lily Flowering Tulip *(Tulipa* 'Elegant Lady')

Thanks to the many talented people who have helped us throughout the development of this book. Two erudite authors shared their invaluable wisdom: David Middleton, who patiently mentored Gail and me throughout the five years we worked on this book, and Debra Landwehr Engle, who advised and edited, created the scrapbook format of the book and wrote the foreword.

Family and friends brought great insight to the process of honing the text. Special thanks to Bill Bohlke, Kevin Bohlke, Leanne Flusser, Margo Jansen, Anne Middleton, David Middleton, Diana Middleton, Douglas Natelson, Kristen Natelson, Anne Perkins, Dick Perkins, Phyllis Perkins, Roberta Perkins, William Perkins and Alice Schaaf. In addition to her assistance throughout the project, Trudianne Melvin provided priceless editing expertise.

Thanks to the St. Charles Writers Group for spending invaluable time critiquing the early manuscript: Mike Balcom-Vetillo, Dave Barrows, Tom Bauerle, Kevin Burris, Elaine Cassell, Paul Cook, Kim Dechert, Stacy Farrell, Fran Fredericks, Bonnie Harm-Pechous, Justin Hoshaw, Kitty Jarman, Joselle Kehoe, Susan Kraykowski, Dean Lundell, Katie Panasi, Dean Pannell, Pat Parker, Todd Possehl, Frank Rutledge, Frank Sobocienski, and Nancy Wedemeyer. A special tribute to Rick Holinger, who read the manuscript once with the group, and then again as an expert reader.

Thanks also to Barbara Ballard, who provided encouragement and perceptive comments in critiquing an early version of the manuscript; Cindy Bohlke, who transcribed many of the interviews with Trudi; Arthur Bradley and Sheri Highland, who helped with business and tax issues; Kathleen Flynn, who helped with computer issues; Bonnie Harm-Pechous, who meticulously edited the first draft of the manuscript; Rich Schell, literary lawyer, who advised us on legal issues; and Mary Carol Smith, Laurie's walking buddy, whose wisdom smoothed the rough spots.

We're so grateful for the expertise of the design staff at Paetzold Associates, whose combined artistic talents created the design of the book. Thanks to Donna, Becky, and Timus Rees; Mindy Holt; Mandy Novotny; Laura DeMasie; and Jennifer Erickson, who shepherded the book through the printing process, and to Kira Henschel and Robin Willard of Goblin Fern Press.

Special thanks and love to our husbands, Bill Bohlke and Dick Perkins, who were always patient and supportive as we created this book.

Laurie Bohlke and Gail Perkins

Container collection on dance floor steps

Gail, more than anyone else, you have inspired me to work on this book. Your artistic and technical abilities to capture images on film are truly remarkable. As a result of your hard work, your pictures are breathtakingly beautiful and must be shared. Thank you.

Thank you also for finding Laurie. Tireless in her enthusiasm for *Trudi's Garden*, she skillfully listened, wrote and pushed me on. No one could possibly be more organized. I know without her, not a word would have been written. All those beautiful pictures of Gail's would have ended up in boxes. My daughters, Trudianne and Margo, would still be pleading with me to write my memoirs.

I owe a special debt of gratitude to Trudianne for tackling my stacks of yellow pads and being the driving force behind the final edit. The encouragement, suggestions, dedication and knowledge from you and Margo helped to make this project worthwhile.

Trudi Temple

Lenten Rose *(Helleborus orientalis)*

Favorite Plants

Trudi's favorite plants have six important qualities:

1.   They do not spread aggressively, either by rhizomes or seeds.

2.   They have beautiful foliage; when the flower is gone, the plant remains attractive.

3.   They are generally resistant to disease and pests.

4.   They don't require time-consuming maintenance.

5.   In the fall, they continue to be attractive by changing color, having a nice seedpod or retaining their foliage after frost.

6.   They are recommended for your growing zone and soil conditions.

garden

Perennials

Anemone sylvestris (Snowdrop Anemone)

Sun or partial shade. Medium moisture.

These pure white flowers brighten up the garden in the spring. The plant spreads slowly and is not particular about the soil. Although it forms small seed heads, Trudi recommends removing the stalks after flowering. Then it will become a neat, tufted ground cover.

Artemisia 'Powis Castle' (Wormwood)

Sun. Dry, well-drained.

This striking plant doesn't bloom and loves dry, sunny areas. The feathery, silver foliage complements all other plants. Trudi also uses it as a strewing herb in her barn, since it releases a wonderful fragrance when stepped on and even helps to keep the mice away. Unless it's extremely well drained in the winter, this Artemisia may not be hardy in Zone 5.

Astilbe chinensis 'Visions' (Dwarf Astilbe)

Shade or sun. Likes moisture.

Trudi can't have enough of this family of plants and loves all varieties. The tall spikes of red, pink or white flowers bloom in summer and don't need to be staked. If they are planted in soil that is loose, moist and amended with organic matter, they flourish. As heavy feeders, Astilbes thrive on top of Trudi pits and will grow in shade or even in sun.

Athyrium nipponicum 'Pictum' (Japanese Painted Fern)

Shade or part shade. Keep moist.

The silvery green foliage of this fern provides welcome contrast to other shade-loving plants. Growing 18" tall, it's ideal for the front of a garden bed. It was named 2004 Perennial Plant of the Year.

Calamagrostis x acutiflora 'Karl Foerster' (Feather Reed Grass)

Sun or part shade. Drought-tolerant.

Place this vertical texture grass between perennials or annuals. It grows four to five feet tall, yet doesn't droop. It provides winter interest and is easy to cut down in the spring.

Clematis paniculata 'Sweet Autumn' (Sweet Autumn Clematis)

Sun or part shade. Medium moisture.

A fragrant showstopper in Trudi's garden for many years, this vine produces clouds of small white flowers by the end of August. Two to three weeks later, fluffy seed heads appear, adding interest throughout the winter months. Birds seek shelter in the thicket of vines throughout the winter. In March, Trudi cuts the whole plant down to twelve inches above the ground. It grows to full height again by summer. Not particular about moisture or soil conditions, it is disease-free. Be sure to provide a sturdy trellis for this rapid grower.

Epimedium x rubrum (Red Barrenwort)

Part to deep shade. Moist or dry.

This groundcover has heart-shaped leaves and dainty spring flowers in white, yellow, pink, purple, or red. There are many species and cultivars; all are worth growing. Early in the spring, use scissors to cut last year's foliage down to the ground. Leaving the old foliage will obscure the flower. As this plant slowly spreads, it chokes out the weeds.

Geranium macrorrhizum 'Spessart' (Bigroot Geranium)

Sun or shade. Wet or dry.

Forming a dense mat, this plant is a hardy groundcover. Delicate spring flowers and exceptionally fragrant leaves make it an asset in any garden. The lobed leaves turn bright red in autumn. Many cultivars are available.

Hakonechloa macra 'Aureola' (Hakone Grass)

Sun or shade. Well-drained.

If Trudi were only allowed to grow one plant, this would be the one. It's her favorite grass because its variegated yellow-green foliage stays attractive into winter and combines well with all plants. "There's no such thing as too many Hakonechloa plants; I love to repeat them throughout my garden," states Trudi. To thrive, Hakone grass needs rich soil. It's easy to cut back in the spring. Allow two to three years for the plant to become spectacular.

Helleborus orientalis (Lenten Rose)

Shade or part shade. Evenly moist, not wet.

This plant has shiny, dark green foliage and bell-shaped flowers that last throughout the spring. Plant in an elevated area, because the flowers have a nodding habit. It does well in alkaline soil and tolerates sun only in the spring.

Panicum virgatum 'Northwind' (Switch Grass)

Full sun. Drought-tolerant.

Growing to five feet tall, this grass stands up straight. It provides texture interest for the winter garden. Use its plumes in dried arrangements.

Polygonatum falcatum 'Variegatum' (Variegated Solomon's Seal)

Shade or part shade. Medium moisture.

The variegated white foliage of this plant brightens up a dark spot in the shade garden. It has bell-like blossoms in spring.

Annuals, house plants and tropicals

Begonia x hybrida 'Dragon Wing' (Dragon Wing Begonia)

Shade or part shade. Keep moist.

This plant is the most profusely flowering begonia, providing vibrant red or pink in the garden. It works well in containers or as a bedding plant. In a protected area, it will bloom until first frost and never needs deadheading.

Brassica oleracea (Ornamental Cabbage)

Sun or part shade. Evenly moist.

Lasting until snow, this plant makes an outstanding fall display in borders or containers. Plants grow easily from seed as long as small seedlings are transplanted directly into one-gallon pots; they're hard to transplant when large. Grow them under netting to limit disfiguring damage caused by the Cabbage Butterfly. It's easier to buy this plant in the nursery in September.

Chlorophytum comosum 'Vittatum' (Variegated Spider Plant)

Sun or shade. Evenly moist.

It might be a surprise to find this houseplant in the garden. The variegated green-white leaves enhance a container or a garden bed. Return it inside for the winter. It's easily multiplied by simply cutting off the baby plants and planting them directly in soil.

Fuchsia triphylla 'Gartenmeister Bonstedt' (Fuchsia)

Shade. Evenly moist.

The trumpet-shaped, orange flowers on this upright plant provide vibrant color as a bedding plant or in containers. One of the easiest fuchsias to grow, it can be overwintered in a cool room. The leaves might drop off in winter.

Iresine herbstii 'Aureo-reticulata' (Chicken Gizzard)

Part shade. Moist, well-drained.

Despite its unappetizing common name, Trudi loves to use this colorful tropical as a bedding plant as well as in containers. She looks for special locations in her garden where this red-leaved plant will be backlit by the rising or setting sun. The low sun makes it appear to be on fire. It is easily dug up before the first frost and overwintered as a houseplant.

Lantana camara (Lantana)

Full sun. Dry, well-drained.

Flowering all summer, Lantanas come in many colors. Be patient, since they are slow starters. Some varieties are prostrate and others grow upright. Over several years, Trudi prunes the upright varieties into free forms, overwintering them in a cool room.

Mandevilla amabilis 'Alice Dupont' (Mandevilla)

Sun, part shade. Evenly moist.

With tubular pink flowers, this tropical vine flourishes as it climbs up a trellis or cascades from a container. Fertilize monthly and don't let it dry out. Trudi hasn't had any luck with overwintering it.

Melampodium cinereum 'Show star' (Hoary Blackfoot Daisy)

Full sun. Drought-tolerant.

This annual forms a large mound of small yellow flowers, blooming continuously from June to frost. A wonderful plant for barren, dry spots, it grows slowly and needs no deadheading.

Solenostemon scutellarioides 'Swinging Linda' (Coleus 'Swinging Linda')

Shade or part shade. Keep moist.

Trudi likes most coleus; this one is her favorite because of the variegated magenta leaves with green margins. The foliage contrasts with all other plants, making it a stunning container or bedding plant. It rarely flowers.

Tibouchina urvilleana (**Princess Flower**)

Part shade. Evenly moist.

This plant, with its royal purple flowers and velvety soft leaves, never fails to attract attention in the garden. Use in containers or as a specimen plant in the landscape. It's a heavy feeder.

Notes

To order this book online, go to www.goblinfernpress.com or to www.Trudisgarden.com.

Trudl is the German diminutive of Gertrud, used by Trudi's family and friends.

All German words are in italics.

We used the Internet and the books listed in the bibliography to determine the botanical names. Botanists sometimes group plants into different families; therefore, the names may change.

The "favorites" section is written from Trudi's perspective as a gardener in Midwestern hardiness Zone 5.

Source for stainless steamer-juicer:

Home Canning Supply, P.O. Box 1158, Ramona, CA 92065, 760-788-0520
www.homecanningsupply.com

Ivy Geranium *(Pelaronium peltatum)*

Market Day

Market Day supports Trudi's commitment to education by helping schools across the country make their fundraising dreams come true. Market Day now serves more than five thousand schools in sixteen states and has raised more than $330 million for education since 1975.

Market Day offers a Family of Fundraisers™, including its flagship monthly food fundraising program, giving parents the opportunity to buy restaurant-quality food at competitive prices through their school each month. Market Day also provides other fundraising options for schools, such as brochure, candy bar and cookie dough programs.

Market Day Gourmet is a home party business providing a special selection of unique foods and kitchen accessories, available exclusively through in-home parties. In keeping with Market Day and Trudi's mission, a portion of every purchase is contributed to a school or worthy nonprofit organization.

For more information about Market Day, visit www.marketday.com.

Bibliography

Purple Coneflower *(Echinacea purpurea)*

Atha, Antony et.al. *The Ultimate Book of Gardening*. Bath, UK: Paragon Publishing, 2003.

Duthie, Pamela. *Growing Perennials*. Batavia, Illinois: Ball Publishing, 2002.

Engle, Debra Landwehr. *Grace from the Garden*. Emmaus, PA: Rodale Press, 2003.

Heriteau, Jacqueline with Cathey, Dr. H. Marc. *The National Arboretum Book of Outstanding Garden Plants*. New York: Simon and Schuster, 1990.

McClure, Susan. *The Free-Spirited Garden, Courageous Gardens That Flourish Naturally*. Chronicle Books, 1999.

Phillips, Roger and Rix, Martyn. *The Random House Book of Perennials*, Vol. I. New York: Random House, 1991.

Phillips, Roger and Rix, Martyn. *The Random House Book of Perennials*, Vol. II. New York: Random House, 1991.

Schlesinger, Arthur M., Jr., ed. *The Almanac of American History*. New York: Barnes & Noble Books, 1993.

Wolfe, Pamela. *Midwest Gardens*. Chicago Review Press, 1991.

Wyman, Donald. *Wyman's Gardening Encyclopedia*. New York: Macmillan Publishers, 1986.

Index

A parting thought

The first motivational speaker I had the privilege of listening to was Dr. James Melton. Of the many wise words he shared, the following still guide me through my days: "Build your life thought by thought, for that is how the world was wrought."

Looking into the future without a dream in your heart is like wandering aimlessly in a black hole. Let's march on in the sunshine with good thoughts and dreams to guide us.

Trudi